**Diverse Gifts**

For Mark
from Ann
with thanks for
your friendship

# Diverse Gifts

*Varieties of Lay and Ordained Ministries
in the Church and Community*

*Edited by*
Malcolm Torry

CANTERBURY
PRESS
Norwich

© The contributors 2006

First published in 2005 by the Canterbury Press Norwich
(a publishing imprint of Hymns Ancient & Modern Limited,
a registered charity)
9–17 St Alban's Place, London N1 0NX

www.scm-canterburypress.co.uk

British Library Cataloguing in Publication data

A catalogue record for this book is available
from the British Library

ISBN 1-85311-696-3

Typeset by
Regent Typesetting, London
Printed and bound in Great Britain by
William Clowes Ltd, Beccles, Suffolk

# Contents

# Foreword

Week after week, year after year, hundreds of thousands of people gather in services of the Church of England. This book not only gives a vital part of the inside story about the people who help this to happen; it also traces some of the living connections between these gatherings to worship God and the rest of life. The Church of England is woven into the fabric of life in local communities and institutions such as schools, hospitals and prisons in remarkably diverse ways, and many millions of people come into contact with its various ministries every week. Some of the people who take special responsibility for both the worshipping life of congregations and the network of other involvements here give their accounts of what their work is about.

I have been very moved by reading it. There is a directness in the writing that brings the reader inside one set of activities after another. Cumulatively it left me feeling both deeply impressed by the description of this 'tip of the iceberg' of the huge amount of dedicated work that goes on year after year and also very grateful for it. It manages somehow to let the richness of ordinary church life become vivid in both its internal and external orientations. It is about life in its dailyness and also at its crisis points. There is deliberately not a great deal of further theological reflection about the shape or significance of the ministries it deals with. Yet time and again I found these chapters resonating with the deepest Christian themes of faith, love, hope, patience, joy, generosity, goodness and gratitude, as well as with the whole range of teachings about creation, what goes wrong with it, and how God's approach of utter involvement in it and commitment to its flourishing works out in the Church and the world.

To have such a rich portrayal of key aspects of church life makes one realize just how inadequate, distorted and even false most images of the Church are in our society. I suppose this is so with most complex spheres of life that have a rich 'domestic' existence, but it does seem to be specially a problem for the Church. Not just outsiders but even committed church members often get much of their picture of the Church from media that almost never get it right, least of all about what it is like to be involved long term. Even when what we receive from the media does not ring true with our local experience we tend to credit its picture of the wider Church that we do not know first-hand. It is therefore all the more important that books like this are available to tell some of the truth about it.

This book will be especially helpful to anyone involved in a local church and who is thinking of ministry in any form. I can imagine it being a good idea for parish clergy, readers, or those in any of the ministries that are discussed to have a few spare copies to hand for lending. But those already in such ministries or who educate others for them will benefit too, and so would anyone who wants to appreciate more fully what the Church is actually like.

Over the years I have found myself undergoing something like a series of conversions to the value of one level of church life after another. This happened with the one-to-one relationship, the small group, the diocese, the national and international levels. The Church is a complex ecology in which all those niches are important. But undoubtedly the one that has most continual significance for me and for most people is the local congregation. Sustaining and developing its life and mission is at the heart of what the Church is about. This book gives a fascinating insight into the people and activities through which this happens, and it also reminds us of the vital complementarity of congregational life with a range of chaplaincy-type ministries in places and to people that often have little connection with a congregation.

Malcolm Torry is to be congratulated for having the idea and carrying it through so well, and the whole team has given in their collaboration an encouraging example of what can happen when God grips people's lives and brings them together.

*Professor David F. Ford*
*Regius Professor of Divinity*
*University of Cambridge*

# Acknowledgements

We would like to thank those many people who have been willing to talk to us or correspond with us as we have prepared our chapters; those who have commented on our drafts (and especially Dr Will Strange for commenting on the historical section in Chapter 1); and particularly Christine Smith of the Canterbury Press for her enthusiasm for this project.

The passage from Lamentations 3 quoted in Chapter 13 is from *The Message* by Eugene H. Peterson, copyright © 1993, 1994, 1995, 1996, 2000, 2001, 2002. Used by permission of NavPress Publishing Group. All rights reserved.

The passage from Psalm 89 quoted in Chapter 9 is from the Good News Bible © 1994, 2004 published by the Bible Societies/HarperCollins Publishers Ltd, UK Good News Bible © American Bible Society 1966, 1971, 1976, 1992. Used with permission.

Otherwise all biblical quotations are taken from the New Revised Standard Version of the Bible, Anglicized Edition, copyright © 1989, 1995 by the Division of Christian Education of the National Council of the Churches of Christ in the United States of America, and are used by permission. All rights reserved.

# About the Contributors

**Ann Atkins** was originally brought up in the Church in Wales. She has attended St Catherine's Church, Hatcham (at New Cross in South London) for nearly 30 years, and has been a churchwarden and Deanery Lay Chair and is also a member of the Southwark Diocesan Ministry and Training Committee. She is an ex-teacher who now works as an administrator for two church-based charities and has an MA in Applied Theology from the University of Kent at Canterbury.

**Liz Newman** was licensed as a Reader in 1999 and serves at St Luke's and St Thomas's, Charlton. A social worker by profession, she is married to Rick and has three teenage children.

**Nick Russell** is a Church Army officer based at the Holy Spirit Church (the daughter Church of St James's Kidbrooke) on the Ferrier Estate in south Greenwich. He and his wife Helen are part of the Ferrier community and work in an ecumenical mission team on the estate.

**Sara Scott** is honorary assistant curate of St Augustine, Forest Hill and Holy Trinity, Sydenham. Sara's first career was as a research biologist. She worked for British Telecom for 15 years as a computer systems analyst and for 14 years as the manager of a general medical practice while simultaneously developing her fourth career as a psychotherapeutic counsellor in primary care. She is now the counsellor in a Church of England girls' comprehensive school. Sara is also a dedicated and enthusiastic amateur artist specializing in ceramics and figurative sculpture.

**Peter Griffiths** has been active in the Church for most of his adult life having fulfilled many Parochial Church Council (PCC) and synodical roles. In 1997 he took on a more overtly pastoral role as a Southwark Pastoral Auxiliary (SPA). He ministers at St Luke's and St Thomas's Charlton, is a voluntary day chaplain at Southwark Cathedral, and serves on the Southwark Diocesan SPA Council as the archdeaconry SPA for Lewisham.

**Arthur Obiora** has belonged to St Catherine's, Hatcham (at New Cross in South London) for most of his adult life. He was ordained as an Ordained Local Minister (OLM) in 1995. He was a magistrate with the Inner London Bench and is currently a manager at the Department for Work and Pensions. He has written *Partnership in the Body of Christ* (Minerva Press, 1998).

**Gillian Reeve** grew up in the Diocese of Southwark and returned there to work in 1972. She is a qualified social worker and while working with a range of organizations has also been committed to being involved with the ministry at St Catherine's, Hatcham, at New Cross. She is also currently a tutor with the Ordained Local Ministry Scheme.

**Cynthia Finnerty** is organist and parish musician at St George's, Westcombe Park, and has lived in the parish for over 20 years. She is a primary school teacher in South East London and a member of the Southwark and South London Association of Organists.

**Alison Seaman** attends Holy Trinity Church, Eltham, where she co-ordinates children's work in the parish. In her professional life she is a freelance writer, trainer and consultant in spiritual education. She has written a wide range of books and support materials for pupils and teachers on religious education and spiritual development.

**Bridget Shepherd** is the Youth and Student Co-ordinator at St John the Evangelist, Blackheath Park, and holds an MA in Youth Ministry and Theological Education. Prior to working at St John's she worked in a local secondary school with young people with behavioural problems, and she has also run a youth homelessness project.

**Malcolm Torry** is Team Rector in the East Greenwich Team Ministry, Vicar of St George's Westcombe Park, chaplain to the Tate & Lyle refinery on Greenwich Peninsula, and Site Chaplain to the new development on the peninsula. Before ordination he worked for the Department of Health and Social Security. Following ordination he was curate at St Matthew's, Newington, at the Elephant and Castle, then curate at Christ Church, Southwark, and industrial chaplain with the South London Industrial Mission, and then Vicar of St Catherine's, Hatcham, at New Cross. He is married and has three children.

**Alison Tyler** is the Chaplain at Wormwood Scrubs Prison in West London. After a career in the Probation Service, during which she was ordained as a priest, she joined the Prison Service Chaplaincy in 1999 and has worked at Her Majesty's Prison (HMP) Brixton, HMP Wandsworth, and Her Majesty's Young Offenders' Institution (HMYOI) Feltham before starting her present job in 2002. She is married with two grown-up daughters, designs and makes textiles and embroidery, and has strong interests in history and the arts. She is a member of the London Diocesan Synod, the Court of Sion College, and The Society of Catholic Priests.

**Paul Collier** worked as a teacher and then a solicitor before being ordained in 1994. After his training on the Southwark Ordination Course he spent eight years as an inner-city parish priest, first as Curate at St John's, East Dulwich, and then as Priest-in-charge at St Hugh's, Charterhouse in Bermondsey. He was licensed as Anglican Chaplain at Goldsmiths College in 2003. He is a member of General Synod where he chairs the General Synod Human Sexuality Group, and has been elected onto the Crown Nominations Commission. He has a particular interest in interfaith dialogue, and in the philosophy of religion. His hobbies include playing the trombone (in Morley College Big Band), cycling and squash. He lives with his partner in Brixton, south London.

**David Flagg** is a priest who is Head of Chaplaincy Services at Queen Elizabeth Hospital in Woolwich. He previously worked in chaplaincy at Burrswood near Tunbridge Wells (where spiritual and medical care are combined) from 1986 to 1994, and at Mildmay Hospital in East London (specializing in HIV care) from 1999 to 2002. Before and between healthcare chaplaincies he has served in parish ministry in Chichester, Oxford and Rochester Dioceses. He is co-author of *A Question of Healing*, Eagle, 1995.

# Introduction

The gifts he gave were that some would be apostles, some prophets, some evangelists, some pastors and teachers, to equip the saints for the work of ministry, for building up the body of Christ, until all of us come to unity of the faith and of the knowledge of the Son of God, to maturity, to the measure of the full stature of Christ. (Ephesians 4.11–13)

In 2003 a group of clergy meeting three times a year to study theology together in the Woolwich Episcopal Area of the Diocese of Southwark gave birth to *The Parish*: an exploration of a number of aspects of the Church of England parish. A consistent thread through the book is that a parish is its community, its congregation, its parish church, and its ministry. Because the book was about so many aspects of the life of a parish (young people, ethnic diversity, ecumenism, pastoral care, art and architecture, etc.) the only chapter specifically about ministry was about the parish priest: the paid full-time priest to whom the bishop gives responsibility for the pastoral care of the parish.

But that is only a very small part of the story, for in the Church of England there are *many* types of ministry in the parishes and there are many types of ministry in institutions such as hospitals, prisons, universities and colleges. Just as there was no book about the many different aspects of the parish, so there is no book about the different kinds of ministry in the Church. This book fills that gap.

In this case the editor rather than a small group has chosen the authors, but from that point on the method has been the same as for *The Parish*. Brief summaries of the chapters were prepared, and then complete drafts. These were then circulated to all of the authors, who met for a day to comment on each other's work and to discuss the content of the concluding chapter. Then the chapters were finalized and the conclusion written. One of the issues we faced was that of repetition. Because all of the authors live in south-east London some contexts appear more than once. Where in the same context different perspectives from within different ministries are offered, we have not regarded that as repetition but as useful diversity.

As with *The Parish*, this is not an objective survey. It is based in south-east London (though it also looks more widely on occasion) and it is written on the basis of the authors' own experience and their consultations with others in the same kind of ministry. We hope that by writing about our own particular situations we shall encourage our readers to reflect on *their* own experience, to make links, and to discover and think about differences. We also hope to see new writing from different perspectives.

Just as this exploration makes few claims to objectivity, so also it does not claim to be a theological exploration. It is about the *practice* of ministry. Sometimes this practice gives rise to theological reflection within the chapter, but we expect the main theological work to be done by our readers. Our task in this book is to provide some raw material on which others will be able to base their own reflections – and maybe their decisions. One of the reasons for writing this book is to provide a resource for people who sense a vocation to a deeper commitment to Christian ministry in some form. Currently there is very little literature to help with such decisions. There is literature about particular kinds of ministry, there are reports on particular ministries from the Archbishops' Council's Ministry Division, and there are leaflets from diocesan training providers, but if a congregation senses the need for additional licensed or other ministry, or feels that a particular person might have a vocation to ministry, then there is no book that explores a wide range of kinds of ministry.

This book brings together in one place contributions from people undertaking a variety of kinds of ministry, and we hope that it will contribute to congregational and individual decision-making.

And those of us undertaking some form of ministry always benefit from talking to other people undertaking similar roles and from reading what others have written – so we hope that what we have written will be of as much benefit to current practitioners as it will be to those who might one day be practitioners.

We have called this book *Diverse Gifts*. As the quotation at the head of this introduction makes clear, diverse ministry is God's gift to the Church. There is a diversity of labelled ministries, and within each one (whether it be labelled 'prophet', 'evangelist', 'Reader' or 'Southwark Pastoral Auxiliary') there is a diversity of gifts, for every practitioner brings something different to the exercise of that particular ministry. As we shall see, while the ministries of priests, Readers, Church Army officers, Southwark Pastoral Auxiliaries, musicians, youth workers and Licensed Lay Workers are all differently accredited, the ways in which these ministries are performed will often overlap, so that we often find similarities between ministries and diversities within them. And of course, every situation brings new demands, so each of our ministries will be diverse and every day we shall bring to them newly diverse gifts.

One of our hopes is that this book will enable its readers to discover the diverse gifts God has given to them and that they will be better equipped to find the right context in which to make use of those gifts.

# 1. Diverse Ministries

## MALCOLM TORRY

Paul and Timothy, servants of Christ Jesus, to all the saints in Christ Jesus who are in Philippi, with the bishops and deacons. (Philippians 1.1)

In Southwark Diocese's *Directory* there is a list of all of the parishes in the diocese, and listed under each parish are the office-holders and ministers. There is the incumbent (or priest in charge, team rector, or team vicar – see the glossary); there are the churchwardens, elected annually by a meeting to which anyone in the parish can come; there are the Parochial Church Council secretary and treasurer; and there are Non-stipendiary Ministers (NSMs), Ordained Local Ministers (OLMs), Readers and Southwark Pastoral Auxiliaries (SPAs). To the uninitiated this is gobbledegook, and one of the purposes of this book is to provide practical explanations of what these terms mean. The purpose of *this* chapter is to provide a historical context and to locate the particular chapters which follow in the context of Church and society today.

The presupposition underlying this book is that *everyone* who regards themselves as a Christian is a minister, a servant of the Church, of their own congregation, and of their community, and that we all have different gifts to bring to this task – hence Ann Atkins' chapter. But to promote its mission, its unity, its worship, its service to its communities, and its other functions, the Church has evolved a variety of labelled ministries. To these particular ministries God calls individuals, and either the individual or their congregation might recognize such a call – and so the selection process begins, sometimes locally, sometimes within the diocese and sometimes locally within the diocese and nationally. One of the reasons for writing about the particular ministries of the Church is to help parishes and individuals to discern the right direction for the vocation they might experience – always remembering that, as at the beginning, the fundamental calling is to follow Christ and to be a servant as he was the servant of all (Mark 10.45).

## As at the beginning

When the day of Pentecost had come, they were all together in one place. And suddenly from heaven there came a sound like the rush of a violent wind, and it filled the entire house where they were sitting. Divided tongues, as of fire, appeared among them, and a tongue rested on each of them. All of them were filled with the Holy Spirit and began to speak in other languages, as the Spirit gave them ability . . . Peter, standing with the eleven, raised his voice and addressed them: 'Men of Judea and all who live in Jerusalem, let this be known to you, and listen to what I say . . .' Those who welcomed his message were baptised, and that day about three thousand persons were added. They devoted themselves to the apostles' teaching and fellowship, to the breaking of bread and the prayers. (Acts 2.1–4, 14, 41–42)

The Apostles preached, people believed and were baptized, and there was a Church. If this event is the birth of the Christian Church then the ministers were there first. But if, on the other hand, a different incident should be counted as the birth of the Church, then there were at the beginning no ministers except Jesus himself:

As Jesus passed along the Sea of Galilee, he saw Simon and his brother Andrew casting a net into the lake – for they were fishermen. And Jesus said to them, 'Follow me and I will make you fish for people.' And immediately they left their nets and followed him. (Mark 1.16–18)

As we read the Gospels we find various ministries emerging: preaching, healing, and exorcising demons; and after Jesus' death and resurrection we find the apostles continuing Jesus' preaching and healing work: proclaiming the Kingdom of God's coming and at the same time declaring Jesus as God's means of bringing about that Kingdom.

As congregations were founded in Jerusalem, Antioch and around the Mediterranean to Rome and beyond, out into Syria, and south into Africa, both activity and structure were needed – and so ministries of various kinds emerged to serve the Church. It was probably all rather chaotic. In Pauls' letter to the Corinthians there were certainly diverse gifts being exercised:

To one is given through the Spirit the utterance of wisdom, and to another the utterance of knowledge according to the same Spirit, to another faith by the same Spirit, to another gifts of healing by the one Spirit, to another the working of miracles, to another prophecy, to another the discernment of spirits, to another various kinds of tongues, to another the interpretation of tongues. (1 Corinthians 12.8–10)

But it is equally clear that there wasn't the kind of leadership structure needed to enable the Church to handle its conflicts, even though Paul mentions 'those who have charge of you' (1 Thessalonians 5.12) and 'overseers and helpers' (or 'bishops and deacons') (Philippians 1.1) – hence the churches' letters to Paul and his responses.

In Jerusalem, a leadership *had* emerged, consisting of 'James and Cephas and John, who were acknowledged pillars' (Galatians 2.9) or of 'apostles and elders' (Acts 15.6). It is this leadership to which Paul appealed during a dispute as to whether Gentiles needed to be circumcized and to keep other parts of the Jewish Law in order to be admitted to the Church, though the evidence here is somewhat contradictory. In Acts 15, a Council at Jerusalem reaches a compromise (Acts 15.19–21), but in Galatians 2.11 and 12 it is clear that parts of the Jerusalem church were still quite keen to see the Law kept and that Gentile elements in the Church were quite clear that it should not be.

Thus, during the first few years of the Church's life there were 'elders', presumably with some governance functions, but there was no uniform pattern and there was no universally recognized leadership; and the congregations experienced a variety of gifts of the Spirit and a variety of functions and recognized some of these by giving them titles. By the time of the (probably later) letter to the Ephesians this process was more advanced: 'The gifts he gave were that some would be apostles, some prophets, some evangelists, some pastors and teachers, to equip the saints for the work of ministry, for building up the body of Christ' (Ephesians 4.11, 12). And by the time the (even later) letters to Timothy and of Peter were written there were 'overseers' or 'bishops' (1 Timothy 3.1–7) and 'deacons' (1 Timothy 3.8–10), and there were also 'elders' (1 Timothy 5.17), though these might have been the same as the 'overseers' and/or 'deacons'.

A tangential part of the history is to be found in the Acts of the Apostles:

Now during those days, when the disciples were increasing in number, the Hellenists complained against the Hebrews because their widows were being neglected in the daily distribution of food. And the twelve called together the whole community of the disciples and said, 'it is not right that we should neglect the word of God in order to wait at tables. Therefore, friends, select from among yourselves seven men of good standing, full of the Spirit and of wisdom, whom we may appoint to this task, while we, for our part, will devote ourselves to prayer and to serving the word.' What they said pleased the whole community, and they chose

Stephen, a man full of faith and the Holy Spirit, together with Philip, Prochorus, Nicanor, Timon, Permenas, and Nicolaus, a proselyte of Antioch. They had these men stand before the apostles, who prayed and laid their hands on them. (Acts 6.1–6)

This group of men appear to be Greek-speaking Christians in Jerusalem (and maybe they were all Jews except for Nicolaus), and their task was to care for elderly Greek-speaking Christians. But to call them 'deacons', 'helpers' or 'servants', is only to offer part of the story, for later (Acts 7) we find Stephen preaching and being martyred for it, and in Acts 8.26–40 we find Philip evangelizing an Ethiopian. These are apostolic functions, and we find little reason here to divide 'elders', 'apostles' and 'deacons'.

As institutions evolve after their first generation or two they develop rational structures or they die. This process may have been first rigorously researched by Weber in the nineteenth century,[1] but what he discovered was no less true of the first and second centuries of the Christian Church. Hierarchy was needed to maintain unity between different congregations in one place, and representatives were needed to maintain bonds of fellowship between churches in different cities. The early churches probably learnt from the ways in which synagogues and other religious and secular institutions governed themselves, but they also found ideas in the New Testament. Since three words were available in the New Testament it is no surprise that a threefold structure of bishop (overseer), presbyter (elder) and deacon (helper) evolved, with the bishop providing oversight in a particular place and relating to other bishops, with presbyters (that is, elders) caring for particular congregations or for groups or functions within a congregation, and deacons assisting bishops and presbyters and sometimes maintaining the 'servant' function of the original Jerusalem diaconate.

The above summary is precisely that: a *very* brief summary of a complex history; and because it is so brief it inevitably misrepresents the history of the first two or three hundred years of the Church's life. The following eighteen hundred years, with different developments in different parts of the world, would be impossible even to begin to summarize. All I can hope to do here is give a brief outline of the history in England.

The Celtic Church had bishops, presbyters and deacons, with bishops such as Cuthbert and Aidan being as much missionaries as church leaders. With the landing of Augustine in the seventh century the Roman pattern of dioceses with clear boundaries took hold, and later on a system of parishes with clear boundaries. By Augustine's time presbyters had become 'priests' and had modelled themselves on the sacrificial priesthood of the Hebrew Scriptures, and subdeacons, exorcists and other elements of an elaborate hierarchical structure had emerged. In England the Reformation of the sixteenth century retained bishops, priests and deacons; but during the Commonwealth of the seventeenth century bishops were swept away and priests became 'ministers', losing any connection with Old Testament priesthood. At the Restoration of the monarchy bishops returned, and the threefold ministry of bishops, priests and deacons was reinstated – and then, during the nineteenth century, the proliferation began.

First came Lay Readers (now simply 'Readers'), licensed to preach and to lead Morning and Evening Prayer but not to preside at the Eucharist: the taking of bread and wine, the blessing of them, the breaking of the bread and the sharing of bread and wine which is the central liturgical action of the Church, presidency of which from the second century had been reserved to bishops and presbyters/priests.

Then came the Church Army, modelled on the Salvation Army but attached to the Church of England and working in its parishes. Licensed Lay Workers followed; and then pastoral auxiliaries of various kinds (Southwark's was one of the earlier schemes).

Parallel to this history is that of the missionary societies, beginning in the eighteenth century. There are already good histories of this movement[2] and I don't intend to repeat any of it here; and because this book is about the Church of England rather than about the Anglican Communion worldwide no chapter appears here on the missionary, a ministry that is still innovative. The Church of England has never established its own mission agencies: both those conducting mission in this country and those conducting mission in other countries have always been the vision of individuals and small groups, and they have remained voluntary organizations, loosely related to the Church of England. (And, after all, what is the Church of England itself but a federation of independent voluntary organizations: the relatively autonomous parishes and some-what independent diocesan organizations.) If a chapter *had* appeared here on the mission agencies' work then it would have been about the increasing numbers of ministers from other countries brought to work here by the agencies, which are increasingly involved in exchange programmes to enable the different parts of the worldwide Church to benefit from its diverse gifts.

One kind of voluntary activity *does* appear in these pages: industrial chaplaincy. The industrial missions, beginning with south London's and then Sheffield's and others, have usually been independent organizations and often ecumenical ones. The denominations have often provided them with person-power and financial resources, but the movement as a whole has retained its independence. But it is an independence for the sake of the Church, as the aim is that as many clergy and laity as possible should engage in the kind of mission activity that relates Christian faith to the world of work and to the economy and its institutions. There are many laity and clergy working in industrial and other institutions or regularly visit-ing them with the intention of relating the Kingdom of God to both the Church and the economy and its institutions, and for this task a certain independence from the Church's own structures is required at the same time as the Church having a responsibility to provide resources for this mission activity.

Another parallel history is that of the ordained ministry

itself. Some of the first presbyters would have been like the
Apostle Paul: non-stipendiary, that is, not paid for being an
elder of a church but rather making their living by their trade
– in Paul's case tent-making. But Paul himself was not entirely
consistent in this matter because we know that although he
wouldn't accept payment from the church in Thessalonika
(2 Thessalonians 3.7–9) he did accept help from the church
in Philippi (Philippians 4.16); and there might early on have
been some elders supported financially by their churches
so that they could give more time to the Church's mission
(1 Corinthians 9.7–12). Slowly the full-time minister emerged
(and there might be a hint of this in the letters to Timothy at
1 Timothy 5.18) – and as the centuries went by such ministers
were to be found in monasteries, schools, hospitals, parishes,
cathedrals, universities, and governments of nation states –
often because they were the ones who could read and write.

As many of these institutions became secular, clergy working in them remained stipendiary, in the sense that they were
paid, but non-stipendiary in the sense that they were not paid
by the Church. Thus a priest working in a comprehensive
school might be paid to teach by the local authority, but that
priest might regard their ministry as related to that school
– so they would now be termed a Minister in Secular Employment (MSE). (Whether someone is called a Non-stipendiary
Minister (NSM) or an MSE seems to be largely a matter of
personal choice, depending on where they see the focus of
their ministry.)

So, ever since a secular institution paid a priest, there have
been non-stipendiary ministers, but from the Reformation
onwards such clergy were not regarded as integral members
of a parish's staff team and no attempt was made to recruit
non-stipendiary ministers for the parishes. This all changed
with the Southwark Ordination Course: a part-time training
scheme for people in secular employment designed to prepare
them for ordination so that they could serve as priests in their
parishes and in their places of work. Thus the modern NSM
was born – though another important part of the story is

supplied by two incumbents in the Kent coalfield who worked in the mines by day and gave their Sundays and spare time to their parishes: a brave but short-lived experiment in modern tent-making.[3]

A part of the story that is still less than 15 years old is that of Ordained Local Ministry. This was, and is, an attempt to return to the beginning, when congregations' leaders were the 'elders', which might mean that some of them were the older, respected members of the community. While there was an element of this in the Celtic Church, and in the Medieval and Reformed churches there were clergy who served where they had grown up, for the past five hundred years the pattern has been one of deployment: someone offers themselves for ordained ministry, they are trained, and they are sent to serve where the bishop thinks they can be useful (though the picture is in practice more complex than this). This is not how it started, and the process as it had evolved was making it difficult for many people to recognize a vocation to ordained ministry because their circumstances made it difficult for them to move – and, in any case, they were already effective leaders where they were. So Ordained Local Ministry Training Schemes were established, and candidates were selected locally, trained locally, and ordained to serve in the parishes to which they belonged. Because this type of ministry is in many ways different from NSM it gets a chapter of its own – and because there is no book about OLM it will soon have a book of its own in the same series as this one.

And then parallel to *all* of these histories is the history of those ministries that have evolved in parishes because the parishes needed them: ministries where selection has always been local, where training has often been according to the apprenticeship model, and where no bishop's licence is either sought or required: such ministries as parish musician, children's church teacher, and youth leader. Because of their importance to the life of our parishes, these ministries get chapters of their own.

Most of our chapters are about *parish*-based ministry

(and non-stipendiary ministry is always parochial even if it is also related to some secular institution). But some places, while being in parishes, are communities in their own right, and the Church has always provided ministry within them: places such as hospitals, universities and prisons. Each of these institutions is a community, it usually has a place for a congregation to meet, it has a minister or ministers, and it usually has a congregation. These places are parish-like, and while the institution might well pay the chaplain, and might well recognize the secular community benefits of having a chaplain rather than regard the chaplain as a president of a worshipping community, the bishop licences their ministries because of their pastoral and missionary importance. They deserve chapters of their own, and they get them.

There are ministries *not* given chapters in this book. This is mainly because the book had to be kept to a reasonable length, but also because of complexities relating to the ministries themselves.

There are still religious orders in the Church of England, and some of them do committed and important pastoral and evangelistic work in the parishes. But a vocation to a religious order is primarily that: it is a vocation to a life of poverty, chastity and obedience. That obedience might involve work in a parish or in some other institution, but that is not necessarily the heart of the individual's vocation. We therefore include no chapter on this type of ministry.

There is nothing on deacons. A major problem is that in the Church of England (and in some other communions) the diaconate has become a probationary year for priests. A new curate is ordained deacon and, if they don't do anything silly during the following year, they are ordained priest. In the period before women were ordained as priests they were licensed as deaconesses (deacons in all but name and hand-laying). When subsequently they were ordained as deacons, though not priests, some thought was given to the meaning of the diaconate; but it is difficult to give positive meaning to an office when for the individual it has a largely negative meaning – for if the deacon was a man then he knew that he was a deacon because he wasn't yet a priest, but if a woman then she knew that she was a deacon because the Church of England wouldn't let her be a priest. Now she can be. (The Roman Catholic Church's permanent diaconate, mainly populated by married men, is also difficult to define positively because the men are married and are deacons because they can't be priests.)

Only when the diaconate ceases to be a probationary year shall we be able to ask ourselves whether there ought to be a diaconate and what its role might be. That time is not yet, so there is no chapter here on the diaconate.

Many congregations have 'worship-leaders' of various kinds. This is a relatively new designation, and it is mainly a means of local recognition of leadership gifts and of a role straddling those of musician and president. The person concerned will often move on to licensed ministry as a priest or as a Reader, and this should probably be encouraged. Some musicians function as worship-leaders, and at all-age services children's church teachers will often take their turn. The term 'worship-leader' might take on a life of its own, in which case a future book of this nature would have a chapter on 'the worship-leader'; but it might continue to overlap with other roles to such an extent that it remains difficult to discern its distinctiveness, in which case it might remain of local usefulness but not be sufficiently defined to enable a generalizing chapter to be based on personal experience.

And then there are people who lead intercessions, people who read lessons in church, welcomers, sidespeople, sacristans, acolytes, crucifers, Bible-study leaders, home group leaders, treasurers, administrators, secretaries, churchwardens, social committee members, people who make refreshments, jumble sale sorters, child protection officers, electoral roll officers, Christmas card deliverers, Christian Aid collectors, flower arrangers, cleaners, churchyard-mowers, and more. There are London City Missioners, Youth for Christ workers, trainers in this and advisers in that – all serving the Church's parishes and in secular institutions, all ministers in one way or another.

To some extent the choice of ministries about which to write chapters is arbitrary (and the order of the chapters is certainly rather arbitrary) as the histories overlap and it is difficult to group the ministries into categories. And the ministries themselves overlap. One week a Reader might preach, then the following week a Licensed Lay Worker, the next an Ordained Local Minister. A priest might lead the children's church, a children's church leader might play the organ, the organist might also be a Non-stipendiary Minister, and the youth group leader might be the incumbent. Yes, there are a few boundaries, particularly in relation to the priest's role, but they are few.

There are diverse gifts and diverse ministries, and they form a complex matrix: for a gift for preaching might be exercised by the musician, and the priest might be a brilliant administrator but not such a good preacher. In the parish or similar institution these complexities are an opportunity, not a problem, for in each place different ministries and different gifts will be differently used – and we shall find that, while there might be a common thread running through every experience of being a Reader, every Reader and every parish will treat the ministry and its tasks differently – which is why any formal job description (now often a requirement) will never be quite right and will always be quickly out of date: for change is ubiquitous, and the configuration of gifts and ministries in a parish will often change rapidly.

In a changing world and a changing Church the different ministries will continue to evolve, and they will be enacted in an increasingly diverse fashion. And we shall see new ministries, and not just that of worship-leader. This will all pose interesting questions for the Church nationally. In the past, the Church's national structures have watched local experiments and then authorized and regulated what seems to be working. This process must continue, and at the same time local experiment needs to be actively encouraged – the only condition being that experiment and its outcomes should be public knowledge. For in this way the Church's ministry, the Church and the world will be enriched – and a future edition of this book will have some new chapters in it.

## Notes

1 Weber, Max, 'The Three Types of Legitimate Rule' (first published 1922), in Etzioni, Amitai and Lehman, E., eds, *A Sociological Reader on Complex Organisations*, 3rd edition, Holt, Reinhart and Winston, New York, 1980.

2 Neill, Stephen, *Christian Missions*, Penguin, Harmondsworth, 1964; Jacob, W. M., *The Making of the Anglican Church Worldwide*, SPCK, London, 1997.

3 Mantle, John, *Britain's First Worker-priests: Radical Ministry in a Post-war Setting*, SCM Press, London, 2000.

# 2. A Variety of Gifts
## The People of God

ANN ATKINS

Now there are varieties of gifts, but the same Spirit;
and there are varieties of service, but the same Lord;
and there are varieties of activities, but it is the same God
who activates all of them in everyone. (1 Corinthians 12.4)

The 3rd July 1977 was a rather momentous day in my life. I
voluntarily attended a church service after a lapse of over ten
years. The reasons for the lapse are not relevant here but the
reason for attending may well be: it was to support a friend.
Five months later, I returned to the same church on Christmas Eve, perhaps in search of something of the true spirit of
Christmas. After that I started going on most Sundays but
was determined not to get involved – sitting at the back and
leaving hurriedly at the end of the service. It must have taken
considerable effort on the curate's part to catch me, but he did
and I gradually became more involved – initially by providing
transport 'because it needed doing'. By doing that, I got to
know people and to learn more about what being a Christian
meant to them. I then started doing more because I wanted to
give something back to the community, which had welcomed
and cared for me. Then, in 1981, I was asked to chair a Christian Stewardship campaign and, to be able to tell others, I had
to look seriously at the principles underlying it. 'All things
come from you and of your own do we give you.' Such gifts
as I have come from God, so I deliberately decided I should

use them in his service. I have a car, others do not, so I can offer lifts; I am a trained teacher, so I can lead study groups; I now have a house with a reasonably large room, so I can offer hospitality. Later still, I started to consider ministry with a capital M and I tried to work out what my ministry really was. I'm still working on that.

So many different forms of ministry will be discussed in the following chapters, but the majority of churchgoers do not fit into those categories. I looked in the dictionary to discover whether the word 'minister' could apply to us too. The noun 'minister' seemed to be applied only to official posts but the verb 'to minister' means 'to attend to the wants and needs of others'. It is rooted in the Latin word for 'servant'. So you do not need to have an official title to be a minister or servant in the Church. The very many references in the Bible to 'servants' or 'service' make attending to the wants and needs of others a very important part of being a Christian.

The Church is becoming increasingly dependent on its volunteers (some of whom are included in the other chapters of this book) as the number of people in stipendiary ministry diminishes at the same time as the number of people attending church regularly (say once a month) is also decreasing. Forty-nine per cent of churchpeople are said to be 'casual', leaving only fifty-one per cent sufficiently regular to be involved in the work.[1]

## What do we do?

I found a list of jobs that need doing in a church,[2] grouped under the 17 headings of administration, audio/visual, bookstall, building/grounds, catering, community service, craft work, evangelism, finance, hospitality, leadership (eg. of groups), pastoral care, publicity, preparing for and taking part in services, social events, support, transport. I will unpack just two of them. Administration: electoral roll officer, typing/computing, photocopying/printing, filing, folding, collating, mailing, surveys and possibly reception/office. Building/grounds:

repairs, decorating, cleaning, laundry, gardening, clearing drains and gutters, maintaining noticeboards. In most churches these jobs are done by volunteers. Many professional and specialist skills may be needed: accountancy/bookkeeping, banking, architect/surveyor, carpentry, bricklaying, general building maintenance, catering, dance, design, drama, electrical, flower arranging, gardening, graphics/artist, legal, library, medical, decorating, photography, plumbing/heating, printing, public address systems/recording, secretarial, teaching. Whatever our skills we should be able to be of use – and just think how much money it would cost if the church had to pay for all that: our financial giving would have to rise considerably. As well as using these skills within the church building and environs, congregational members also represent their church on the boards and synods of the wider church and on secular committees.

I questioned members of my own church and deanery about what they do in and for the church.[3] They were doing a wide variety of jobs from being a churchwarden to copying the notices, serving on the events committee to selling Traidcraft goods, reading lessons to washing altar cloths and most of them were doing several tasks, one person listing 21 jobs. They do say that if you want to get a job done, ask a busy person. I also asked them if they had a Christian ministry outside their church, in their everyday life. General answers included 'laborare est orare' (to work is to pray), 'all forms of interaction in the world are a form of Christian ministry' and 'trying to exemplify Christian love'. More specific examples included advocacy on behalf of people with special needs; encouraging and supporting friends and family; hospital visiting and 'making elderly people happy'. 'Truly I tell you, just as you did it to one of the least of these, you did it for me' (Matthew 25.40). It seems that most of us do try to carry our Christian principles into our daily life and work. One particular married couple from my church, now deceased, not only both served in the church itself in many ways and for many years but were also extremely active in local politics, living out their faith in that world. Just one person suggested that it was possible to have a profound Christian life that does not impinge on society or the church. I think that cannot be true. I believe that being a Christian means being in community and cannot simply be a personal thing.

## Why do we do it?

I also asked people why they worked so hard in these ways, and surprisingly few mentioned religious reasons. Answers were much more related to a sense of community, of belonging. If you join an organization you should contribute to its functioning in whatever way you can. Some like 'being involved' or 'knowing what is going on.' Some answered more simply 'because it needed doing', 'because it's something I'm good at' and 'for pleasure'. One person quoted the Book of Common Prayer communion service (quoting Matthew 5:16): 'Let your light so shine before men that they may see your good works and glorify your good Father which is in heaven' as the ideal to which we should aspire. Maybe we should not be concerned about what people say about their motivation but assume that it is God-driven even if they don't know it – or maybe we should encourage more introspection and discussion about our Christian ministry. I too have done many different jobs in the Church over the years, although I would probably now identify my particular gifts to be in the fields of administration and leadership or teaching. Throughout that time my motivation has varied.

## The time to do it

The mathematicians reading this will have noted a span of 27 years in my story between returning to church and the present day, and I am reminded of the well-known words from Ecclesiastes 'For everything there is a season and a time for every matter under heaven: a time to be born, and a time to die . . .' (Ecclesiastes 3.1–8). Time has much to do with ministry. The amount of time laypeople have to devote to church work will vary throughout their life: making a career, bringing up children and caring for elderly parents may all limit the amount of time available; being young and single or being retired might increase availability. Perhaps more importantly, time can be considered in relation to development. Looking at my own example – I began with the very practical offer of transport, but later felt able to take part in and then lead discussion groups and begin to share my faith. When I was unemployed for three years I had time to offer my administrative and organizational skills. It is important to consider both aspects of time when thinking about the ministry of church members. First, the amount of time they can realistically spare and then the stage on their Christian journey. Although, for example, a young, new Christian may have a fair amount of spare time, it would be unreasonable to expect them immediately to take on a teaching role. It is also important to remember that as we progress along the path, we can challenge ourselves and others to take on more demanding roles (always remembering that we will probably need to give up something else to take this on). The person I mentioned earlier, who listed the 21 jobs she currently does, could perhaps have relinquished the flower-arranging or coffee-making when taking on a preaching and teaching role. To be fair to her, she did suggest that those of us who do a lot may frighten off others who could do some of our tasks just as well.

Older people who have been very active in church life may begin to feel that they are regarded as useless when they are no longer able to do the catering, cleaning or collecting for Christian Aid. We, and they, need to acknowledge the contribution they have made over so many years and recognize the contribution they can still make. They now have time on their hands, which those of us who are so busy do not have. They have time to listen and to pray – both considerable contributions to the church community. They have experience to offer and can tell the story of their Christian journey to those just setting out, encouraging them along the way.

I thought it interesting that only one of the people I asked about their ministry talked about money. She spoke of giving to the Church and supporting people and organizations outside it. Some laypeople (and of course clergy too) give sacrificially for the upkeep and work of the Church. At a particular time in their life this may be the only support a person can offer, but it is a form of ministry without which our churches would not survive and it should therefore be acknowledged and appreciated.

## Our mission – the way forward

Moving from the specific to the more general, I would like to look at how the Church treats all these volunteers who work so hard for its mission. People today are less willing to volunteer, either in church or elsewhere, than they used to be. More and more we are a society of people who find it difficult to commit ourselves, and this difficulty is not going to go away. However, it does still appear that churchgoers volunteer more than others, and we need to encourage and support them.

Life has become more hectic for all of us, but the Church could not function without its volunteers, so how can we recruit and retain them? Currently there is much talk about 'being a missionary church'. Bruce Saunders[4] writes of the parish as 'a Community in Mission', and says that Christian ministry is by nature collaborative and has a sense of purpose. He defines mission as 'the Church's willing partnership with God in God's own purpose for creation'. If we accept that this is what we should be doing – not simply preserving what we have and nurturing those who belong, but looking outward, being disciples of Christ, showing the love of God to people who have not yet recognized him (as well as to those who perceive him differently) – then we have a better starting point for considering the ministry of all people than my earlier list of jobs. We complain that a few devoted laypeople 'do all the work'. We say: 'We've tried everything to get more people involved but they won't be.' Perhaps we should approach the matter from a different direction.

As we have seen, people work for the Church for a variety of reasons, but usually feeling that they *ought* to contribute something to the organization they have joined. People with enthusiasm for a vision will much more willingly make a contribution to its fulfilment. Let us forget about the long list of jobs that need doing and start further back, with developing together, priests and people, a common vision for our parish church. We are the Church, the body of Christ: there is no 'them' and 'us'. We are in it together.

We need to create a vision to which we can all enthusiastically give our support, and we can then work out a mission plan for how it can best be achieved. 'What do we want to achieve?' 'Why do we want to do that?' 'How can we achieve it?' and then, 'Who will do what?' At this point we should realize that to achieve our mission purpose everyone can, and should, contribute to that mission, using our God-given gifts in his service. Into the mission plan can be inserted the good cleaners, the financial experts, and the carers. The gifts of everyone can and should be used. (Who knows? The vicar may not be the best evangelist or a woman the best cleaner.)

At this point we would need to identify the gifts, skills and availability of all members of the congregation. It would be worth spending some considerable time on this and doing it carefully. When I asked people what they were good at, several said 'Nothing'. One of them is a legendary cook, another a great raconteur, another always has time to listen. When another was asked what she saw as her real ministry, she said 'pastoral care', but she was actually doing committee work. People would need to be encouraged to recognize their own gifts – with no false modesty – and these gifts then need to be matched to what needs doing. Then we can move purposefully to implement our common mission plan. At this point we do need to be careful to avoid making assumptions – for example, that someone who teaches all week will want to teach Sunday School, or that an accountant would like to be treasurer (although some may). Our daily job is not always our chief talent and, even if it is, we may want a break from it one day a week.

Our reason for involving laypeople in work for our common mission is of course not simply to 'help the vicar who is doing too much' and prevent her/his collapse through overwork. It should be much deeper: an equal sharing of our common vision and a respect for the gifts we all bring to the task. 'For as in one body we have many members, and not all the members have the same function, so we, who are many, are one body in Christ, and individually we are members one of another' (Romans 12.4, 5). St Paul continues with a long list of possible gifts. There is no question of a hierarchy of gifts but instead an emphasis on mutual dependence. It is not necessarily better to administer the chalice than to serve the coffee – just different.

The mission plan may to some churchgoers seem very business-like and therefore to them 'not how the church works', but I think we can learn from the business world. Mission statements and business plans are now an everyday part of our secular work life. Let us take the best from the secular world and use it to God's purpose. A parish church's mission plan for the year would need to cover at least three areas: the congregation; those who might enter the church; and the general community. If members of the congregation are to proclaim the gospel, they must be encouraged to learn and be supported in their faith, so members of the congregation need to nurture each other. If people who enter the church are to stay or return, they need to be made to feel welcome and valued. That means showing an interest in them, giving hospitality, and being able to share our faith in a non-threatening way. Mission to the community and to the world is not just about proselytizing or even necessarily about speaking the gospel. It is about demonstrating it by, for example, feeding the hungry, visiting the prisoner, comforting the sick, and standing up for the oppressed. This can be done in the family, at work, through charitable giving or work, or through overt political action. The church's mission plan must contain realistic objectives for what can be done in the wider community in a particular period of time and by whom.

The other good thing we would need to take from the secular world is the idea of regular evaluation. Which of our objectives have we achieved, which need to be 'rolled over' and, possibly, which should be abandoned as currently unworkable? It would be easy to have good ideas and fail to carry them through, to continue doing things because we've always done them, or even not to recognize the fact that we have actually achieved that objective and need to move on to the next step.

In our secular work we are usually given a job description and training of some sort. In the church we expect people to jump straight into a job without knowing clearly what it entails and to do it well. Training is haphazard. I needed to have someone show me how to clean the silver properly and one of the older members did that. I needed to attend a course about Parochial Church Councils (PCCs) before I could offer similar training to others. If we can offer training to laypeople we will be able to recognize *potential* as well as *ability* and to encourage and develop it. (An incidental bonus may be that individuals gain skills and experience which can feature on their CVs and be of use in their paid work.)

Many secular organizations offer 'support and supervision' to their employees, helping people to reflect on how they are doing their job, whether they could do it better, and what would help them to do that. The Church of England supports its clergy through their Annual Review, but we offer nothing of the sort to the many laypeople who are working within our parish churches. Some may be feeling taken for granted. Yes, they are doing a good job and we appreciate it (even if we seldom tell them): but do they want to go on doing that job for ever or do they need a change? Are some people square pegs in round holes and need to be moved on tactfully? I am not suggesting formal interviews, but if perhaps we put jobs into groups, with a person responsible for each group, then regular opportunities could be made for this sort of conversation, thus avoiding some bitterness and disaffection.

The most important things we can do for our church and for each other is to value each person, not primarily for what they *do* but for who they *are*. To do this we need to know each other well, recognize each other's good qualities and celebrate them and, most difficult, accept each other's failings and live with them. Quite often you can see on a weekly news-sheet or in the parish magazine something general like, 'Thanks to all who contributed to the harvest flowers and arranged them so beautifully.' We do not often say 'You sang that solo beautifully' or 'You've really made the silver/windows/floor gleam – thank you' or 'That was a really good sermon.' If we are all to work together on our mission plan then we need to be mutually supportive and encouraging. To summarize: to sustain the church's work we should have a clear common purpose (and realistic objectives), recruit carefully and offer training and support and, most importantly, show people we value them and their contribution.

Let's look at a typical Anglican congregation. There will be a few high-profile laypeople with obvious roles, such as the treasurer, PCC secretary, musician; a large number who do less noticeable things such as regularly washing the purificators, cleaning the church, working in the garden, attending community meetings; and one or more accredited ministers. There will be the 'casual' 49 per cent. And there will be a sizeable number who appear to do nothing except come to church at least once a month. Are they simply 'receivers' rather than 'givers', not contributing to the common purpose? I don't think so. First, we all need to receive as well as to give. Without spiritual sustenance from the church it is difficult, if not impossible, to continue to give to it. Without that sense of the numinous I received on that Christmas Eve so long ago, I would not now be doing what I do. Without regular spiritual nourishment, I would not have the strength or patience to go on doing it. Second, these people who 'do nothing' are part of our church. Just by being there they make a contribution to the worship, which nurtures us all: they swell the singing, give volume to the Amen, and increase the weight of prayer, a contribution we should value. Third, when we get to know them as individuals, we may find that they do have a Christian ministry, not in or even for the parish church, but elsewhere. It may be at work, for example in one of the caring professions or in education; in the family, bringing up young children or caring for ageing parents; among neighbours, visiting regularly, delivering meals, telephoning, offering emotional or financial support; in the community, as members of organizations that 'feed the hungry' or 'visit the prisoner'. They are being Christ in the community and that too should be a valued ministry. In their case our duty as a parish church is to give them the sustenance to perform that ministry – by loving concern and encouragement, by prayer, by making the services they attend as spiritually uplifting as possible, and by seeking to equip them with the theological tools to deepen their ministry. We should not heap guilt upon them because they do nothing 'for the church'.

Clergy, Readers and Southwark Pastoral Auxiliaries have pieces of paper signed by the bishop that not only authorize their ministry but also put a value on it. We too, the vast majority of church members, the footsoldiers who keep the show on the road, can probably also find a piece of paper that authorizes and values our ministry – our baptism certificate. Through baptism we are valued members of the Church and Christ's servants in the world. 'Christ has no body but yours, no hands but yours . . .' St Theresa of Avila). On the whole, we do gain great personal satisfaction from serving God and our community and from doing the job, however mundane or boring, as well as we can. However, we do sometimes also need human recognition, encouragement and, occasionally, thanks. Priests and people need to be mutually sustaining if the Church is to grow both spiritually and numerically into the twenty-first century. A common vision will take us forward. We can rephrase, 'What do we want to achieve?' as 'What is being a Christian all about?' Being a disciple, following Christ, being as Christ-like as possible, however you define it, that is the duty and the joy to which we are all called as ministers.

Teach me my God and King
In all things thee to see
And what I do in anything
To do it as for thee.
A servant with this clause
Makes drudgery divine.
Who sweeps the room as for thy laws
Makes that and the action fine.[5]

## Further reading

Chapman, Christopher and McKinnon, Jill, *God Has No Favourites: Encouraging Equal Opportunities in Church Life*, Southwark Diocesan Board for Church in Society, London, 2001.

Cole, John, *How to Be a Local Church – An Action Plan for Every Christian*, Kevin Mayhew, London, 1990.

Croft, Suzy and Beresford, Peter, *Getting Involved: A Practical Manual*, Open Services Project & Joseph Rowntree Foundation, London, 1993.

Edmonds, Lesley, *Volunteers – A Resource for Your Church*, The Volunteer Centre, Berkhamsted, 1988.

*Using Volunteers, a How-to Guide*, Administry, St Albans, Vol. 1, No 4, now available from Matters Arising, 62 Farm Road, Rowley Regis, B65 8ET, telephone 0845 128 5178.

## Notes

1 Benson, Paddy and Roberts, John, *Counting Sheep: Attendance Patterns and Pastoral Strategy*, Grove Booklets, Nottingham, 2002.

2 Administry Mini Guide 4, *Discovering Gifts and Skills*, Administry, St Albans, 1997: now available from Matters Arising, 62 Farm Road, Rowley Regis, B65 8ET, telephone 0845 128 5178.

3 My thanks to them all.

4 Saunders, Bruce, 'Purposefully Going: The Parish as a Community in Mission', in Torry, Malcolm (ed.) *The Parish*, Canterbury Press, Norwich, 2004.

5 George Herbert (1593–1633).

# 3. Making Connections
## The Reader

LIZ NEWMAN

Let all things be done for building up. (1 Corinthians 14.26b)

## Taking the first step

When my vicar suggested that I should consider becoming a Reader, he made me re-engage with a possibility that had occurred to me to varying degrees since I was a child: what about the idea of me in some sort of formal ministry? I had always dismissed it before for two main reasons. One reason was to do with my perception of myself, that I wasn't good enough. The other reason was to do with my perception of the Church – that if you got sucked in too far, you'd lose all ability to relate to people on the edge or outside. Piety frightened me, so did irrelevance. I wasn't at all sure that throwing my lot in with the Church of England wouldn't condemn me to both.

This new challenge from my priest began to shift my first problem of self-belief. (Some of us need those who are able to discern what we might have to offer in order to kick start us into making a right response to God. We need people to believe in us as God believes in us but, because of the damage we've sustained in life, we find it hard to accept that God believes in us.) Resolution of my first problem made me reconsider the second one. Were my fears about this deeper commitment to the Church really justified? When I came to think about it, I'd been surrounded for about 15 years at St Luke's, Charlton by enough examples of people who were deeply within the Church but had also managed to stay 'on the edge' with integrity. Maybe I'd be able to manage it too. I didn't have any defence any more.

## Training

The training was a big commitment and a challenge to my life/work balance. At times this new vocation was in competition with my vocation as a mother. I was afraid my children would see the Church or, worse still, God, as a rival for my time and love. I didn't always get it right. I remember a friend of mine on the course contemplating the paradox that, under stress, with deadlines looming, she'd told her child to go away and leave her alone because she was trying to write an essay on love! For me it has been especially difficult when my children got to the age when they started to question God's existence and the Church's relevance to them. How much of this rebellion might have been a working out of resentment of the 'thing' that took a lot of Mum's time and attention? No doubt some of it was. But I know as well that they feel good that I got involved in something that's bigger than just our family. Families are usually the people who know us best, warts and all, and so our homes are the places where we're most strongly challenged to 'walk the walk' if we're to 'talk the talk' with integrity.

I struggled a little during my training with the sense that I didn't quite belong with this group of people who called themselves Readers. It never quite felt like they were 'people like me'. It was probably my fear of becoming 'too churchy' reasserting itself. There was also the age factor. I was younger than your 'average' Reader when I started training. When I was a teenager, there was a Reader on the staff team of the church I attended. I know anyone who is over 30 looks positively ancient to most young people, but I'm pretty sure he was in his 60s when I knew him. Lovely as he was, I would never in a million years have considered that ministry then.

He was an elderly man. I was a young woman. No matter how much we hope to be able to communicate across difference, I think it's inevitable that we're more likely to end up in ministries where we see 'people like me' represented. I'm glad that work is being done to attract younger Readers.

The teaching was exciting, improved my confidence in my theology, and helped me integrate understanding and experience. But although Readers are trained for a ministry within their parish, the training I received was not really tailored to the setting where I'd be carrying out my ministry. Yes, of course we need to get inside the contexts from which the Old and New Testaments emerged, and in which doctrine developed. I love doing so and the course provided us with valuable tools to help in this process. But the sense we make of all our knowledge in the context in which we carry out our ministry, and the way in which our people will hear the sense we try to make of it, must take into account the unique stories of the places in which we live and worship. This would be my main criticism of the training I received at the time. We can acquire knowledge, but how we communicate what we learn: well that's a whole different issue that I wish we could have given more attention to.

## Lifelong learning

At the end of a quite gruelling three-year course, when I often didn't feel that I'd got the life/work balance right, I was extremely glad that I could draw a line under that episode in my life. Foolishly, I imagined that, having got that course under my belt, I could exercise my ministry for the next 30 years on the strength of it. But our society as a whole seems to have come a long way in recognizing the value of life-long learning, of breaking down barriers between the teacher and the taught, and of embracing instead the reality that we learn as we teach and we teach as we learn. The dangerous thing, I'd say, is to believe that we've done our learning. We must never come to believe that there are places, experiences or people we can't learn from. It didn't take me long to realize how wrong I'd been in thinking I'd 'finished'. The Christian Faith is a living, breathing faith and unless we live and breathe it, and constantly grow and develop in our engagement with it, then we'll dry up and have nothing to offer to God's people. Five years after finishing my course I'd say I never want to stop 'training'. As a licensed Reader, I have ongoing opportunities for training and mutual sharing with others.

Vital too, of course, is the continued development of our relationship with God. A profound truth I've come across in the time since my Reader training is the need to distinguish between the concepts of *building* the Kingdom and *witnessing* to it.[1] I tend to be a bit of an activist and so I have to watch myself, because activists can lose sight of the truth that what we're called to do is to join God in the work he is constantly doing, not to see ourselves as the initiators of that work. Being able to see my ministry as an opportunity to *witness* to God's Kingdom and not as a responsibility to *build* it helps me to guard against getting absorbed into frenetic activity where I can become unreceptive to what God is saying to me. It is a constant reminder to me that God is the origin of all that is good and that we are not. To join in we need to be open to God's presence and activity all around us, and that means we have to try to walk with God each day. Spiritual direction has been an invaluable support to me in this journey.

## Ministry at the interface: bringing the world into the Church

'A Reader's particular contribution to the Church is to see the secular world through theologically open eyes; to bring this experience to the life of the Church and to apply a spiritual dimension to the secular world.'[2] So the church acknowledges particular value in being at the interface between the secular and the sacred. Having experience of employment or other work in a secular setting can be a valuable asset for Readers. But this isn't a gift that Readers alone have access to, as it

might have been in the past. Increasingly, Anglican clergy
are non-stipendiary and may well have secular employment
as well. There are clergy in close relationship with the life of
their wider community and in frequent contact with people
of all faiths and none. Equally, there are Readers whose lives
revolve so much around their church that it's hard to know
where they derive any experience that allows them to relate
faith to non-church life. So it's up to Readers to stay at the
interface: it doesn't happen automatically.

## Preaching and teaching

I've always been aware of what a huge responsibility preaching is. I love the whole process of crafting a sermon. While
sermons are created for others, they can also give the preacher
a fantastic opportunity for spiritual growth and reflection. I
need to plan and reflect carefully about what I'm going to say
because I'm that sort of person. Others will offer their best
through being more spontaneous. I'm lucky to find myself
supported and led by those who believe in the importance of
personal integrity and of being true to one's self in preaching.
I've learned not to try to be someone I'm not. It's OK to be me,
not a clone of someone else.

Before training I had questioned the whole concept of
preaching. My work experience was about facilitation. Having
a captive, apparently non-participatory audience was an alien
experience. What right did I have to set myself up in a position
of authority? I also didn't see myself as a public speaker: I
wasn't someone who sought the limelight. Gradually I began
to understand that this was less to do with me, more to do
with how my God-given gifts, and the way in which my life
experiences had both helped and harmed me, could all be
used to nurture others. Course input on preaching released
me from fears because it stressed preaching from a position
of vulnerability. This made sense to me. I believe it's only by
allowing myself to become vulnerable in preaching that I
allow God to unlock what might be of use to others.

Authorization boosted my confidence and self-esteem once I was able to let it seep into my self-understanding that I was speaking with the authority of God's Church. I might have questioned my own qualifications, or my right to preach, but the Church, which I respected and loved, had made that powerful statement in authorizing me. The responsibility I felt heavily, but the trust was liberating.

For me, work and home life is always a rich source of material and inspiration for preaching, teaching and pastoral care. For instance, I have used my one-time tendency to retail therapy to wonder why we look to materialism to satisfy a hungering for God. I've used recollections of the birth of my children to reflect on the wonder of God's incarnation in Jesus. I've used the permission children are now given to trust their own feelings, rather than to respect their elders, in order to ask whether we can become dependent on our leaders in a way that inhibits the growth of our own relationship with God. I've used experiences of bereavement to try to help us get inside the minds and hearts of the disciples on the first Easter Sunday. Lives we lead and the lives we're brought into contact with, when intermingled with Scripture and the traditions of the Church, enable us to make those connections and bring the Word of God alive in our context.

## Pastoral care

Reader ministry is described as pastoral, but the existence of Pastoral Auxiliaries in Southwark and the fact that there are no pastoral duties that are exclusive to Readers (although Readers can take funerals on completion of additional training) means that there is often little connection between Reader ministry and pastoral care. But I think it's nonsense to imagine that we can draw a line between the pastoral and teaching or preaching. First, if our sermons don't make pastoral sense then they will run the risk of irrelevance and insensitivity. Second, when we lead worship, teach or preach, we are inevitably seen as leaders within the Church and sometimes therefore as people who can and will respond to the needs of others. It's the experience of many Readers that congregation members will seek them out for emotional or spiritual support, and we need to be able to respond, or certainly to facilitate some response. Third, we forfeit the right to exercise a leadership role unless we're prepared to share in and care about our fellow parishioners' lives. So the 'pastoral' part of my ministry is less formal and defined, but it is certainly there.

## Blurred boundaries?

There are things I do that I might not immediately think of as an outworking of my Reader ministry: things like organizing youth activities. What's happened is that my training and experience as a Reader have built my confidence to initiate and take on work like that, but I still don't categorize such work as part of my Reader ministry. So when the Readers in my benefice are asked to create and lead a special piece of worship, that's something easy to identify as being carried out with my Reader hat on. But what about starting up a parent and toddler group in the church? Is that the sort of thing a Reader would include on their annual returns to the diocese?

Maybe I tend to be too compartmentalized in my thinking: certainly other Readers regard a broad range of activities as an expression of their ministry. This brings me back to a blurriness that sometimes feels uncomfortable. If an activity doesn't require you to be a Reader to do it, if there isn't any 'gate-keeping' that judges who is and isn't 'qualified', then am I acting as a Reader or just doing what countless non-accredited Christians do all the time?

There are sometimes issues as well about involvement of the non-accredited in leading worship. I believe this is a very real dilemma for some and a difficult one to deal with both emotionally and spiritually. Readers may regard it as good news that many members of the congregation want to participate in leading worship, and to teach and offer pastoral care. And yet it inevitably poses questions. 'What then is distinctive in my ministry as a Reader?' 'What is three years' training worth if it's our baptism, or our level of commitment, that's now being used as the yardstick for who can and does take on leadership within the Church community?' The worst scenario is that we end up feeling we have to compete for space to exercise our ministry. Perhaps this is a by-product of living in a Church that formalizes some ministries but also advocates 'all member ministry'.

This can all be rather difficult in parishes where Readers like tidy role descriptions. And any ministry faces difficulty if the minister feels vulnerable. Sometimes Readers can feel 'sidelined' after a change of incumbent. Others feel the exercise of their ministry is totally dependent on the value attached to it by their incumbent and if this isn't high then they may consequently struggle to recognize their worth or importance.

The way forward would be to see Reader ministry in a creative way, not as a prescribed role with a finite number of opportunities for expression. Maybe our particular training in linking the Word and the world could help us to discover new opportunities for teaching and pastoral care in their broadest sense. There are other possibilities for flexibility too. Vocations leading to authorized ministry don't develop in consistent patterns across God's Church. Authorized ministers in places where vocations have been flourishing may find themselves carrying some guilt when they become aware of parishes with fewer human resources. Readers do get invited to preach in parishes other than their own, to fill in or help out or because they have a particular connection. Occasions such as Women's World Day of Prayer provide opportunities for ministry within other parishes. There are some who would dearly love to see Readers having a chance to develop this flexibility further. These issues challenge our understanding and definition of 'our church' and its parameters.

**Ministry at the interface: bringing the Church into the world**

My experience has been that this ministry is seldom understood by those outside the Church of England. The title 'Reader' itself does little to enlighten about the content or nature of the role. Unchurched friends, family and colleagues would have said my training and authorization proved I was a 'religious person', but they had no prior image of what a Reader was or represented, whereas they would all have definite ideas and reactions to the priestly ministry. This has led me and others to the conclusion that Reader ministry, certainly outside the Church, has an indistinct identity. What you *do* as a Reader is more obvious in the context of a worshipping community where you will have a visible leadership presence.

So we may need to work hard to find an expression for our ministry outside our faith communities. But opportunities do arise. Some Readers feel that their authorized ministry is recognized and even respected in the workplace and community and that this in itself is the catalyst for many opportunities to witness to faith. If the Reader's secular role is such that it allows 'easy connections' to be made, for instance, teaching religious education or working for a Christian project, then opportunities for ministry can be clear-cut. Leading worship at school and chairing the management committee of a faith-based project are both activities Readers I know have got involved in.

If the work or community setting has no Christian basis, there are still possibilities a Reader can develop. There are Readers who have contributed to the development of ethical work policies and practices, or who share their faith in the staff room or socializing with colleagues. I was invited to talk about my faith to a group of primary school children in my daughter's class. Readers local to me have been invited to speak at a local hospice's Christmas service.

Yet I haven't always found it easy to find ways of 'bringing the Church into the world'. My training enabled me to reflect on links between 'world and Word', but I don't feel I emerged from the course as well equipped to address faith in secular contexts as to preach in church. The former is more nebulous and less definable, I know; but I would have felt more confident in making these links between faith and life at work or in the community if questions like 'What do we want to achieve?' 'How do we negotiate secular/faith boundaries?' 'How do we express faith to an unchurched audience?' and 'How do we expect and find God's activity everywhere?' had been explored further. Maybe all Readers can do is to understand that the process of working out exactly what their ministry could mean in the secular contexts in which they find themselves is an ongoing, even a lifelong, one.

My current paid employment involves me running parenting groups for (usually) mums with children under the age of 11. Recently I've done this with a group of about 12 young mothers living in a particularly deprived area of south-east London. Some of the issues they face are domestic violence, low educational attainment, clinical depression, and material poverty. They are people I can only describe as having been battered by life. And people who have been battered by life have a few options open to them, one of which, it seems to me, is to become emotionally hardened, to survive by pushing feelings to one side. It isn't the best recipe for sensitive, responsive parenting, but maybe it's a way of getting by. So how do I link the secular and the sacred among this group of women to which Reader ministry means absolutely nothing? I believe the most powerful thing I can do is to treat them with respect. It is to turn up week by week, to try hard to recognize the pain behind what can be impolite behaviour, to listen to them, to help them try to find solutions to their problems, and to help them discover their love for their own children – a love that often gets hidden beneath all the stress; and in all of this to communicate that they and their children matter. Each and every one of them is made in the image of God and is loved by him, although I'm unlikely ever to use those words.

In the secular context, we cannot always be vocal or overt about our faith. Although I've worked in faith-based voluntary organizations for the past eight years, their ethos has always ruled out proselytizing. In these organizations, acts of support, kindness, solidarity, challenge and healing are understood as declarations of the gospel in themselves, and in offering them I have always believed myself to be witnessing to God's Kingdom. Michelle's story might help to illustrate this.

Michelle's husband was recently deported to West Africa. She is the single mother of three young children. Michelle spent most of her teenage years in care and was imprisoned during her second pregnancy. Listening to her story, I've heard very little evidence of the sort of factors that set people on a road towards success, social acceptability, or stability. Time and again her experience has been one of rejection and disappointment, and understandably she now finds it hard to trust, hard to hope that there could be a better future. Yet she now also has three young children totally dependent on her, and her greatest fear is that her children will grow up to resent her in the way she resents her own mother, fracturing relationships for another generation. My involvement is to help her acquire some skills, knowledge and awareness that will put her in a better place to meet her children's needs. I believe this work is witnessing to God's Kingdom and proclaiming the Good News. But how?

First, by working with families like Michelle's, I believe we demonstrate Christ's bias to the poor and the vulnerable.

Second, Jesus made the blind to see and the lame to walk. God cares for the whole person and so we need to do this too. When we work on setting boundaries for the children, managing difficult behaviour, or potty training, what's being declared is that the whole of life is holy ground. We should not elevate the spiritual as the only aspect of our lives that God cares about or works through.

Third, people who have very little are often the most vulnerable to accepting societal norms about what constitutes a 'good life'. Children are mercilessly targeted by advertisers who use them to indoctrinate parents into the belief that food must be entertaining not nutritious; that clothes must be a certain brand to be acceptable; and that toys must be expensive, battery-operated and linked to TV programmes or films. Parents can be left feeling inadequate if they don't pander to these consumer-driven ideals. So Michelle's flat is full of pink and purple plastic toys she can ill afford. Gently, I help her to ask herself whether her girls really need all these things by helping her understand that the most important gift she can give them is her time and attention. I understand this as counter-cultural witness to God's Kingdom – and a challenge to the idolatry that lies behind consumerism and exploitation, an idolatry that distorts our understanding of what is of real value in life.

Lastly, I am addressing some of the things that can act as barriers to faith. It has always struck me that the person with low self-esteem might find it harder to accept their preciousness in God's eyes, that the person who has rarely experienced generosity without strings attached might find it almost impossible to believe in God's unconditional love, and that the person whose failings have resulted in rejection and abuse might not be able to hope for forgiveness. My task is to help Michelle and her children to catch a little of the reality of who they are in God's eyes. My job is not to bring Michelle to faith in Christ, but the work done with her declares God's love for her and thus proclaims the gospel.

I might be acting like any Christian social worker would in this situation. I might be acting like any non-Christian social worker. Because I am a Reader, though, I have had the privilege of a training that helps me to make sense of my secular employment within the context of God's activity and to interpret where and how God might be at work in all of this. Perhaps Michelle's story will turn up, disguised as it is here, in one of my sermons.

## Some conclusions

Martin Jones describes the gift of reconciling sacred and secular as 'bringing together what centuries of sloppy spirituality and church culture have falsely separated'.[3] My attempts to reconcile the sacred and the secular have led me to the conclusion that, in the end, the distinction between sacred and secular is false because God is as much at work outside the Church as inside it. God cannot be limited. This is what people outside the Church need to hear if they are ever going to be able to recognize God's touch on their lives. People inside the Church need to hear this if they are going to recognize God at work all around them and join in. Our work as Readers is about showing the 'unchurched' that God isn't locked up inside the walls of our churches but is at work wherever there is compassion and justice. Our work as Readers is about helping our congregations to live Christian lives in the secular places they find themselves in, rather than suggesting that they have to be in sacred places in order to live Christian lives.

After my first sermon someone thanked me for not 'talking down to us'. This said a lot to me about an expectation that learning, titles or status open up gaps between people, leaving some as 'experts' and others feeling inadequate. This would be the complete opposite of what I have come to believe my ministry is all about. I am hugely privileged to have had the input I have had from the Church and yet I often feel we get the balance wrong. The Church seems very ready to highlight and celebrate the authorization of the few. The only way it's OK to invest in the few, it seems to me, is if the few use what they have to empower the many, not to promote themselves. The best way to empower the many is to do our best to make the gospel come alive, to treat it as the Good News that it is for the people we live, work and worship among.

When I was welcomed by my parish after my licensing, I remember saying something along the lines that this wasn't about me but about all of us. I didn't articulate it well at the time, and maybe it's only experience since then that has shown me what I really meant: that what I offer is only of use to God if it enables others. With authority comes responsibility, and ministry must always ultimately be about service.

In my Certificate of Admission to the Office of Reader, I'm described as 'our beloved in Christ'. They strike me as beautiful words. No matter what tensions and unresolved issues there may be in my Reader ministry, in the end it's about the working out of love. My only response to the God who first loved us, the God who calls me beloved, is to offer back what I can by loving and serving those parishioners and others with whom I am privileged to share my life.

## Further reading

Logan, Pat, *Witnessing to the Kingdom: Church, Gospel and Social Action,* Diocese of Southwark, London, 2003.
Harries, Richard, *God Outside the Box,* SPCK, London, 2002.

## Notes

1 Logan, Pat, *Witnessing to the Kingdom: Church, Gospel and Social Action*, Diocese of Southwark, London, 2003.

2 *Guidelines for Incumbents and Readers,* Southwark Association of Readers, London, revised February 1999.

3 Jones, Martin, 'No work no mass', *The Reader,* vol. 98, no. 3, p. 11.

# 4. A Different Kind of Soldier
## The Church Army Evangelist

### NICK RUSSELL

There are varieties of services, but the same Lord; and
there are varieties of activities, but it is the same God who
activates all of them in everyone. (1 Corinthians 12.5, 6)

At 9.30 at night on New Year's eve, a knock on the door was
followed by a young voice through our letter box: 'Nick! Open
the door. We've got John with us and he's been attacked!'
There on the walkway outside our flat was John, congealing
blood obscuring one eye and spattered over his face, hands
and coat. He was flanked by two teenagers. 'We found him
on the staircase. Someone attacked him.' John was clutching
a can of beer in one hand and a bloodstained box of party
poppers in the other. He staggered in, leaving a blood stain on
the wall as he steadied himself. We thought he must have lost
an eye, or at least that his eyelid was in shreds. His story was
that he had gone to spend New Year's eve with friends, who
had let him down, and that he had been set upon while having a beer on one of the communal staircases. He alleged that
another youth we knew had been among his attackers.

My wife Helen sat him down, grabbed a towel and got him
to press it over the affected area. We called an ambulance and
the police and went with him to hospital. His main injury
turned out to be a hideous gash over his left eye that left a fold
of skin drooping. It took about an hour to clean it and stitch
him up, and X-rays revealed no further damage. We arrived

back home at about 3.45 a.m. to the sound of outrageously loud music from a nearby flat, not for the first time. They finally turned it down after being threatened with being reported to Environmental Health.

The Ferrier Estate where we live and work is made of grey concrete tower blocks and six-storey squares. It has about 1,900 homes and has a black and minority ethnic community which makes up close to 60 per cent of the residents (my former career as a linguist can be quite helpful!), and includes refugees from a number of countries. The caretakers work hard, but fight a sometimes losing battle as communal rubbish chute rooms are piled high with smelly waste and stairways are used for taking drugs, and also as lavatories. Graffiti is a way for young people to assert their ownership of the area. There is an atmosphere of resignation and heaviness that you get used to and don't notice until you come back from more pleasant surroundings. There is vandalism and crime, high unemployment, many young mothers struggling to bring up toddlers on their own, and social exclusion with illiteracy and low educational attainment.

The morning after the incident (New Year's Day) the mother of the youth who had been accused arrived, distraught, at our front door. Her 12-year-old son Jack had been arrested and spent the night at Plumstead police station. I took her there. After a cigarette to calm her nerves, we went in, only to find that the police had taken Jack back to the estate. John had withdrawn his police statement. Meanwhile, Jack had arrived at our flat where Helen gave him toast and tea. His alibi seemed good, and he was holding back tears, clearly shaken up by the late night arrest and detention. We became convinced that John had made a mistake identifying him on a dark staircase with a large amount of alcohol inside him. Other youths mentioned Geoff, another teenager we knew as a small-time drug dealer, as the assailant. Perhaps John had owed him money. Later, however, John was adamant that Jack had been there, even if he had not been part of the attack.

Geoff had been a member of a youth club that met in our

flat, but had got into a lot of trouble and had problems at home. He has been in and out of care and secure units. On one occasion, he knocked on our door at 7 a.m. When we opened the door, bleary-eyed (it was our day off), he announced that he had run away from a care home with £90, which he proposed to spend on drugs. He had previously stayed in the home of a dealer, and we feared he would return there and put himself in danger. Helen phoned the police, but they didn't come until three hours later, by which time Geoff had sensed something was up and left. He went to live in a squat, but there was no heating and nothing to cook on. Three days later Helen bumped into him, and he came back to our flat with Jack for something to eat. While Helen prepared some food, I negotiated between Geoff, social services and the police to get him to agree to go back into care.

The upshot was temporary care accommodation in Woolwich. Jack insisted on coming with us to take Geoff there. Helen drove. I turned around in the car to see Geoff preparing an enormous 'joint', using up the last of his cannabis, as he explained, to steady his nerves, before going into an environment where drugs would be hard to come by. We could not allow him to smoke his 'blaze', but had no means of stopping him without calling the police, which would have caused him to run away, and be at large once more. We stopped the car, and he got out and crossed the road, saying he would come back after he had finished his joint. However, relaxed by the drug, he breezed back over, still smoking. Jack got out and argued for a share. At this point, a police car drove slowly past, stopping 200 yards down the road. Headlines flashed into my head: 'Church Army officer in youth drugs scandal!' I thought of my credibility and the work on the Ferrier Estate crumbling, but the police car moved off, and we delivered Geoff safely back into care.

Geoff is an illustration of the main reason young people engage in anti-social behaviour on the Ferrier. Like others, he is a victim of an inter-generational cycle of family dysfunction, whereby young people suffer from abuse, neglect, rejection, parents who are addicts, and a poor home life, which causes them to identify with their peer group rather than with their family. In turn, they become unstable parents and bequeathe a damaging emotional legacy in the way they relate to and treat their own children.

In an area that is stigmatized and where there is a lot of lovelessness, love has to be demonstrated in relevant action before people will begin to understand the love of God, let alone accept the gospel. A strong focus of the mission on the Ferrier Estate is youth work among damaged young people, not only for their sake, but also because they cause most of the crime and vandalism, which acts as a depressing backdrop for people on the estate. In helping to reduce this problem, the quality of life of many is improved. Helen and I work both on our own account and with Greenwich Youth For Christ, who have a major project on the estate.

Jack comes from a large family: 11 brothers and sisters. There have been five different fathers, creating a family with intense inter-sibling conflict, with a mother overwhelmed by the task of bringing them up. His father sees him occasionally, and buys him expensive clothes and trainers, vital to a young person's status on the estate. He drops into our flat, ditching a hard mask and becoming for a short while a normal 12 year old, enjoying games and harmless fun.

The mission team's practical expressions of love to him and many others who have scarcely any experience of adult affirmation and attention are the best way to convey that they are precious children of God. They desperately need time and affection given by adults, all too rare in an environment where the peer group (and earning a high position through crime and vandalism) is the main way troubled young males combat low self-esteem. The help given to John by the two teenagers was in itself a miracle of transformation. Lenny, the first, had been involved three years before in pushing lighted newspaper through our letterbox. Earlier in the year the second, John, had tried to mug two volunteers from the visiting Soul in the City mission, punching them in the face, as well as being involved in numerous other crimes. We have learned that, by the patient love of God channelled through the mission team, damaged and violent young people can be changed.

'Superkidz' is a children's club run by my wife based on a model used in the Bronx. It attracts an average of 60 children every week to an event with games, drama, wacky worship songs, and ethical teaching from the Bible. Three times a year parents are specifically invited to events, which attract 200–300 people. About 300 homes are visited each week. It has become a huge sign, alongside the mission's drop-ins, youth work, and family outings, of the love of God and his practical involvement in bringing some joy into difficult lives. Badging an activity with the Superkidz badge gives it instant credibility in the Ferrier community.

The Ferrier Estate is home to many addicts. Emaciated heroin users are part of the group that uses the church for drop-in sessions. Crack cocaine is also common. Many are psychologically dependent on cannabis. Alcoholics are part of our lives. Almost invariably as we get to know them a painful life-story emerges. Steve, an alcoholic who stayed with me for a few months, never knew his father, was abandoned by his mother at an early age, and then as a teenager lost his only brother in a joy-riding accident. Highly intelligent, excellent company and with a good knowledge of psychology, he is crippled by a profound despair and has no will to give up alcohol.

A sense of powerlessness and fear comes from routine and frustrating struggles with benefits and other bureaucracies (a very common example being late payments of housing benefit leading to letters threatening eviction), and the estate's 'regeneration' scheme has left us with an even greater sense of powerlessness. Most of my work as Chair of the Ferrier Residents' Action Group (a job I keep trying – unsuccessfully – to relinquish) is defending residents' interests as the estate is emptied by phases, demolished and rebuilt by private developers as a housing association estate. It will end up more than twice as big, with two-thirds of the homes privately owned (and a net loss of social rented housing). The initial impression given to residents in a crucial survey was 'new homes for old'. However, what has become apparent is that, instead of waiting for permission to build suitable new housing on open land for Ferrier residents first, around 650 households are being moved into existing social housing stock, in many cases in a worse state than their Ferrier homes, and invariably smaller, since the Ferrier properties are 10 per cent larger than usual. The only costs being reimbursed are removals, reconnections and replumbing of household equipment, postal redirection, and only *half the second-hand value* of carpets and curtains that don't fit the replacement homes. (There is no compensation for furniture – sometimes still being paid for on hire-purchase agreements – that is too big to fit the replacement homes.) Attempts to get a fair deal for residents has required asking numerous questions at public Council meetings, sending press releases, and writing letters to higher bodies. There have been angry exchanges with councillors, officers and government civil servants. At the time of writing the Local Government Ombudsman is investigating, and horror stories of lives blighted by the dispersal of support networks and enforced moves to unsuitable homes keep coming to me.

Christian mission is perhaps better placed than any other approach to help this deprived community, because it contains a unique emphasis on love and the preciousness to God of each individual, because of its emphasis on loving one another, and because we can rely on the power of our healer God and his relevance to the major problems in people's lives. Christian love has to be practical to be convincing. Providing enjoyable activities like simple minibus trips to the seaside or coach trips to adventure parks make an important impact. Writing official letters to the Council, or character references to courts, or letters to creditors from Helen's Debt Advice Centre, help to assuage anxiety.

For a lot of people, low self-esteem is a crippling problem, so we use every opportunity to preach a God for whom each individual is intrinsically precious and infinitely valuable and to give people a direct experience of being regarded and *treated* as infinitely valuable, unconditionally. A sense of fear and insecurity have often been inflicted at an early age through harsh family environments, and the violence that is part of the estate's youth culture. More seriously, there is experience of what the psychologist John Bowlby would have called a false Internal Working Model: a set of unconscious assumptions (in this case negative) formed in infancy about relationships. They cause relationship break-up in adulthood, and weaken the ability to build a life. The unchanging love of God channelled through members of the mission can alter people's internal working models, particularly at those times when a person would expect patience and care to run out. The effect is most clearly seen in young people, whose negative internal working models are typically reinforced when they result in anti-social behaviour, which in turn leads to hostility and rejection from others. Changing their internal working model enables them to enter a positive cycle of better behaviour, which is rewarded by acceptance and approval, which makes for increasingly positive assumptions about other people's attitudes.

Vital to this process are drop-ins. Drop-ins have to be safe environments, both physically and emotionally. Both those for adults and those for young people are quite heavily staffed, so that an ethos of love and acceptance predominates. A large and aggressive person who comes into the adult drop-ins and likes to start arguments has to be skilfully diverted by staff members; and there is the would-be evangelist who irritates people so much that he has to be intercepted by someone who is prepared to spend most of the session listening to obscure and confusing theology.

In this kind of safe environment people gain confidence and can be 'real'. They can have a try on a computer, or express themselves through art. We had the enormous benefit at one time of a Roman Catholic helper who is trained in psychotherapy and enabled people to use art as a means of expression. One day a lady with mental health problems who hardly ever spoke a word sat down to draw and paint, revealing a tragic world of fear and anxiety. Both her children were in the process of being taken into care.

Our hope for everyone we meet is that they will find healing and fulfilment in their own relationship with God: the supreme therapeutic relationship, and (to put it in Bowlby's terms) the securest of all attachments. We have found that a model that works is the one summed up in the words:

- *Blessing* – bringing various kinds of help and good experiences freely to individuals and groups, as an expression of the grace of God.
- *Belonging* – the team is a community that welcomes and cares for people, and encourages them to feel they are valued and have a place in the group (whether or not they share Christian beliefs).
- *Believing* – some of those who belong will respond to the love of God with a desire to follow Jesus.
- *Behaving* – being a Christian allows the power of God to regenerate and heal, and carries with it a desire to conform to Jesus' ethical teaching, so that transformation takes place.

Several Christian organizations are working together on the Ferrier Estate. Eltham Green Church, based nearby in Westhorne Avenue, pioneered the mission, and continues to be major suppliers of people and financial support to most of the mission activities. Early on I suggested the need for an expression of church geared to the estate's non-book culture, and Eltham Green Church took up the challenge. In a remarkable way the drop-in for adults run by Esme Robinson (also from Eltham Green Church) has acted as a stepping stone to this. Then there is the Greenwich Youth for Christ Praxis project providing among other things drop-ins with activities, and information and communications technology (ICT) facilities. There is Holy Spirit Church: a shopfront behind which there is space for a small congregation to gather. Recently we have been joined by a gifted young couple: Holy Spirit Church's new Baptist minister, Charlie Ingram, and his wife Sarah, who is a qualified youth worker with previous experience on the Ferrier Estate. St James's Church, our mother church, supplies expertise in the form of its capable rector and congregation, and the lively and enthusiastic help in Superkidz from its young people. And of course there is the supportive and long-suffering congregation of Holy Spirit Church, with its services frequently shattered by troubled youths!

Through all of this work the church is beginning to be seen as relevant to a community that a few years ago felt alienated from it. The mission team is giving people a truer picture of a God who cares *and acts* in their situation. This approach to mission is producing a notable impact (especially on young people). It also bears fruit in a new congregation, 'Ferrier Friendship Tea', where people have moved from indifference or hostility to the gospel to a warm-hearted willingness to hear it – and in some cases to embrace it. In particular, there are two recovering alcoholics for whom relationship with God is the decisive factor in their liberation – something we only dreamed of in the beginning.

## The Church Army

The Church Army was founded in 1882 by Wilson Carlile, who started life as a successful businessman and became a clergyman in his thirties with a passion for reaching the poor. The organization he founded is constantly adapting to ensure that Carlile's vision of reaching people for the gospel where they are – outside the Church – is the main thrust of its work. The work we are doing on the Ferrier Estate is precisely the kind of work that Carlile would now be expecting his Church Army to be doing. And the Army is active in other ways in similar areas. Andrew Payne was a member of an Area Evangelism focus group, training and equipping members of various churches in a diocese to share their faith and move forward in culturally relevant forms of worship. Chigor Chike works with refugees and homeless people in London, in projects offering church buildings as night shel-ters on a rota basis, and training opportunities for refugees with support from the local Council. The specialist elderly people's work includes Chris Crosskey's ground-breaking work for Alzheimers sufferers. He helped them to worship, and a specialist Christian Alzheimers organization has published some of his material.

They are all called 'evangelists': not only because that's what Church Army officers are commissioned as in the Church of England, but also because that's what they are: bringers of good news.

Church Army is fully behind the thrust of *Mission-shaped Church*, a Church of England report that explores the many different ways in which we can be the Church today. Increasing numbers of officers are involved in fresh expressions of church where unchurched people can feel comfortable. Ferrier Friendship Tea on the estate is 'church', but in the style of our drop-in. Its strong focus on social interaction based around tea and sandwiches and cakes, followed by Bible study, prayer and singing, is quite different from the long-established morning service.

Church Army has numbers of people engaged in other 'fresh expressions of church', including officers who work in night clubs, where they 'do church'. This kind of evangelism is an integral part of the training given to all new Church Army evangelists. But the Training College, where most of this training occurs, is more than an educational establishment. Close attention is paid by tutors to the personal qualities of evangelists. The (often terrifying) First Year Report details weaknesses as well as strengths, and these are revisited in the writing of the Final Year Report, by which time they are supposed to be a thing of the past. The development of personal qualities in the Church Army's evangelists is essential because most people look at the messenger before they will consider the message. The college places a strong emphasis on placements and working out a theology for particular contexts and problems for it is in particular communities that people hear the gospel and respond to it.

Church Army posts are advertised either through the head-quarters bulletins or in the press, and are applied for in the usual way. They tend to have funding for three to five years. The Evangelist Support Scheme is a means for individuals, trusts and churches to contribute towards the stipends of individual evangelists, and travelling around 'preaching for our supper' in various churches has become part of our lives, with the added benefit of making the Church Army more widely known. Helen and I are extremely grateful for a great deal of financial and prayer support from friends and churches as well as other funders. Our hope is to continue to specialize in estates ministry, and we are undertaking study to this end (Helen in urban mission through the Holy Trinity Brompton Regeneration Trust's School of Urban Mission and myself through Open University psychology modules).

John, the alcoholic who staggered into our flat on New Year's Eve, has now been through detox, and has been guided by other team members into a Christian rehabilitation centre. Faith has appeared in him like a tender shoot. We hold our breath and pray that God will complete his rescue.

## Further reading

Mission-shaped Church: Church Planting and Fresh Expressions of Church in a Changing Context, Church House Publishing, London, 2004.

# 5. Balancing Roles
## The Non-stipendiary Minister

### SARA SCOTT

You remember our labour and toil, brothers and sisters;
we worked night and day, so that we might not burden
any of you while we proclaimed to you the gospel of God.
(1 Thessalonians 2.9)

I am a priest and I am a woman. I am also, at various times,
and among other things, a mother, a wife, a daughter, a
counsellor, an artist, an organizer of arts events, a student, an
employee, an employer and a volunteer. As a priest I am self-
financing and am therefore both a Non-stipendiary Minister
(NSM) and a Minister in Secular Employment (MSE).

## How I became a priest

For many years of my life I wanted to have nothing to do
with God. I grew up in a non-churchgoing family. My three
brothers, two sisters and I all went to the local Church of
England primary school. Confirmed at 13 I, like many other
teenagers, stopped going to church in 1964 at the age of 15.
For the next 25 years I studied biology, worked as a systems
analyst, married, had one child and divorced, became a trade
union representative and Labour Party activist, remarried,
had two more daughters, began training as a humanistic
and psychodynamic counsellor, managed a GP surgery, saw

patients for counselling, and had no religious affiliation. I
entered into the world of psychotherapy as client and trainee
at the age of 36. This was an absorbing and often painful
experience but through it I came to realize that I could not
rely solely on myself for hope and happiness.

I had formed an idea that the goal of humanistic psychotherapy was to achieve wholeness and happiness through
'self-actualization' or 'self-realization'. I imagined that this
was something that happened through one's own efforts.
I travelled as far as I could down this road and found that
moments of euphoric happiness were followed by loneliness
and despair. Just when my thoughts were particularly gloomy
I had a 'Road to Damascus' experience. I was walking along
the road near my home (I live on top of a hill in south-east
London with views across the whole of London) and thinking
about how every separate person in the whole city was living
a life that was intrinsically unconnected to anybody else. I
was troubled by thoughts of the meaninglessness of it all if
we simply live and die in the pursuit of individual happiness.
Suddenly and unexpectedly I felt filled with a sense of being
loved. The only way I could make sense of the feeling was to
attribute it to God and to accept that I was experiencing the
presence of the Holy Spirit. I understood at that moment that
we are all connected to each other and to the planet and to
every other living creature, not directly one to another but
through God, the creator God who encompasses the universe,
and God the Holy Spirit, the breath of God who flows through
us all. The shock of this revelation woke me up to a spiritual
hunger in myself that I had been denying.

I began to search for a church in which to worship and since
I had been confirmed in the Church of England it seemed right
to start at my local parish church. I was 42 years old and had
not been a member of any church for 27 years.

Within a short time I responded to a call to ministry
and with help and encouragement from many people I was
ordained priest ten years later.

## Training

As a mature ordinand with family responsibilities I trained at Southwark Cathedral on the South East Institute for Theological Education (SEITE) course. This is the successor to the Southwark Ordination Course (SOC) that trained the first Church of England Ministers in Secular Employment. A strong sense of this history remains, but by the time I started training the Southwark course had already merged with the Rochester and Canterbury courses. The course provides the same training for ordinands who will become stipendiary ministers as it does for NSMs. Other students who were not ordinands attended the evening classes but not the residential weekends. One difference between the candidates for stipendiary ministry and those for non-stipendiary was age. Each diocese has different rules for the age at which candidates can be selected for stipendiary ministry. I started to train when I was 48, which meant that I was considered too old to train for stipendiary ministry.

The training course lasts three years, with an evening class each week at one of the three diocesan centres, seven residential weekends a year and an annual ten-day residential school at Easter.

## Background to non-stipendiary ministry

Non-stipendiary ministry in its modern form in the Church of England emerged relatively recently. St Paul wrote of financing his living expenses as a missionary by continuing his trade as a tent-maker, but the first official non-stipendiary Ministers in Secular Employment were ordained in England in 1963, having trained on the Southwark Ordination Course set up by Bishop Mervyn Stockwood. These pioneers were 'worker priests'. By 1983 there was a network of 15 part-time training courses offering training for ministry to ordinands who continued to pursue their secular work and live at home.

A significant proportion of Southwark's clergy are non-stipendiary. It is now unusual for a parish to have a paid curate. The normal pattern of stipendiary ministry is for a training curacy of three years with an experienced priest followed by appointment as vicar or priest-in-charge of a parish in which there are no other paid ministers. In a career of 30 years of ministry only one tenth of that time will be spent as a curate. This means that most curates are volunteers, whether they are classified as NSM, OLM (ordained local minister) or PTO (retired priest with permission to officiate), and none of these is going to move on to become the priest in charge of a parish. Of the 192 ordained women in Southwark Diocese (March 2005) 62 are in stipendiary parish posts and 105 are NSMs, OLMs and PTOs. The others are employed as chaplains in educational and healthcare institutions.

## My first experience of ordained ministry

On completion of the SEITE diploma course in the year 2000 I was ordained deacon at Southwark Cathedral and sent to Holy Trinity, Rotherhithe to serve my title (the training period following ordination). Ordination as a priest followed in 2001. Rotherhithe is a place that has experienced great change in recent times. From the poverty of an area dependent on casual labour in the docks it has been transformed into an inner-city dormitory area for young city workers. Property prices are high but there is little disposable income. Older people with memories of the past live alongside young professional incomers and recent arrivals from various African countries. All of these groups were represented in the church community. My home is only 15 minutes' drive from Rotherhithe but I had little previous knowledge of the area. (Neighbouring areas of London differ greatly from each other. I have lived in Blackheath and New Cross and worked in the City and in Deptford.) I had few preconceived ideas about Nonstipendiary Ministry in a parish that I did not live in but thought that I would be able to be involved to a greater extent than turned out to be the case. My paid work occupied more time than I had expected because I became Acting Practice Manager for 15 months at a time when I had planned to reduce my commitment. My vicar was unfailingly supportive but I think it was hard for him as well as for me to define a satisfactory job description outside Sunday worship. I found myself feeling guilty because I was not contributing more, but uncertain about what else I could do.


## My current post

After three years in Rotherhithe I was ready for a new challenge and in May 2004 I was licensed to the parishes of Holy Trinity, Sydenham and St Augustine, Honor Oak.

Geographically the parishes to which I am licensed as Honorary Assistant Curate share a common boundary and together form a banana-shaped area stretching from the north-western end of Sydenham, through Forest Hill to Honor Oak and extending to the southern edge of Peckham Rye. Holy Trinity is a traditional evangelical parish; St Augustine's is in a time of renewal having been closed for more than a year following the retirement of its previous vicar. My own church background is in a liberal catholic tradition. Between the two parishes the ministry team consists of one full-time priest in charge, one Ordained Local Minister (OLM), one newly licensed Reader and myself. The OLM and the Reader are both licensed only to Holy Trinity.

The two parishes are separate so each has its own PCC. The main parish service at Holy Trinity is in the morning while St Augustine's has only an evening service at present. Both churches have some Sundays when the main service is a Service of the Word rather than Holy Communion. I assist with and lead services at both churches on Sundays, preach, attend two sets of PCC meetings and deanery meetings and sometimes officiate at funeral services.

Coming towards the end of my first year at Holy Trinity I am finding similar difficulties regarding my role as I experienced at Rotherhithe. With most parish activity happening on

Sunday, and not living or working in the parish, most of my involvement in the parish is with existing church members on Sundays.

But St Augustine's has the potential to be different. The parish needs to find both a congregation and a mission. The parish has no mid-week church-based activities and it has a very small regular congregation. The church building is located in a woodland area at the top of One Tree Hill. This is a problem for people who have difficulty walking or are nervous of the dark, but it is a glorious place for concerts and for quiet days. The location is part of the reason the church closed when it did. St Augustine's currently has only evening services. The congregation has built up slowly and decisions need to be made about whether to start holding services on Sunday mornings. If morning services start I shall be responsible for services more often as they will be concurrent with services at Holy Trinity.

Despite our hopes for the parish our ideas may have to be re-thought as a recent survey report has created new uncertainty about the future of the building as a parish church. Many structural problems have been identified and we do not yet know what the consequences will be. Parish life is full of issues such as this, and they can involve the non-stipendiary minister just as much as the stipendiary minister.

### Minister in Secular Employment (MSE)

Although I perceive much of my ministry to take place in my workplace I do not often tell my counselling clients that I am a priest. Having worked in a general medical practice for many years I now work two days a week in a girls' comprehensive school near the Elephant and Castle. I am employed as a counsellor and not as a chaplain, and the girls need to be able to talk to me without preconceived ideas about what is or is not appropriate to tell a priest. As a counsellor in a GP surgery I developed skills in recognizing when 'God talk' would be helpful and when to avoid it.

My past experience of work in a variety of different sectors and my continuing employment affects the way I carry out my role as a parish priest and the way I am perceived by parishioners as does my unpaid work experience as a woman and a mother.

## Finding support as an NSM

NSMs can suffer from a rather haphazard structure, which can fail to provide support and direction appropriate to their particular form of ministry. All newly ordained deacons and priests are supervised in their training post by the incumbent of the parish to which they are licensed. While the parish priest may have worked in a secular job before ordination, they are now paid by the church. Non-stipendiary ministry ought not to be a cut-price way of staffing a parish but a distinctive ministry with its own characteristics. Newly ordained Non-stipendiary Ministers who continue in secular paid employment may have no role model or mentor to help them develop a ministry in which all aspects of their lives have value.

I have a fantasy of the archetypal curate being a young man in his twenties, enthusiastic and innocent, being sent out to tramp the streets day after day visiting parishioners in their homes and learning to be obedient to the rule of his seniors. Ministers employed in secular work have a very different experience. Priorities have to be assessed and the result is often permanent feeling of guilt. Work and family have to take first place followed by church duties. Time for reading, reflection and spiritual refreshment is hard to find. There is little opportunity to conduct funerals or to take school assemblies or visit people in hospital. There is unlikely to be time to develop a habit of saying the morning and evening office with another person. The NSM's competing priorities may result in the training incumbent feeling reluctant to ask for more than assistance with Sunday services and feeling disempowered when exploring the nature of their curate's ministry in the workplace.

For stipendiary parish clergy, deanery chapters can be one of the most useful mechanisms for meeting other local clergy, but chapter meetings are not always helpful for NSMs, especially when they take place in the daytime and when most of the discussion relates to issues relevant to incumbents.

Southwark Diocese had a network of consultation and support groups. These groups were open to clergy and laity, Anglicans and members of other denominations, but were only useful to a minority of NSMs as they required a commitment of 90 minutes a week for three 10-week terms. The groups encouraged 'reflective practice' in that the material discussed would be the day-to-day problems that everyone encounters, looked at objectively without blame or guilt but with an aim of reaching a deeper understanding. I belonged to one of these groups from 1992 to 2002 and it was extremely important in my formation as a priest. I then co-facilitated one of the groups for four terms until the scheme closed at Easter 2004.

Diocesan 'Oasis' days are designed specifically for MSEs. These take place on Sundays once or twice a year and can be very useful. They are one of the few opportunities for ministers who are trying to find a balance between paid secular work and unpaid ministerial work to meet and share their experiences. They are also a time when senior diocesan clergy can be invited to share in the concerns of MSEs. However, many MSEs do not come because they are in parishes where they are providing cover for one reason or another, or have so few free weekends that they are reluctant to use one to meet more clergy.

It would be good to have opportunities for more regular discussion of the issues that we encounter, be they personal, theological or in relation to our ministry in parishes and workplaces and to have a communication channel for expressing our collective concerns to the senior clergy in the diocese, and it would be useful for every NSM to be assigned a more senior NSM as their mentor. This would be someone who continues to experience the conflicts inherent in the role of being an NSM and who would be able to help someone to discern the particular way in which their calling as a priest might be expressed.

## What is it like for me, being an NSM?

Being a Non-stipendiary Minister has its positive side. Being unpaid gives me some freedom to choose what I spend time on. I am a volunteer, so I can give priority to my paid work and also to the needs of my children when necessary. I can take time during the week to attend classes in ceramics and sculpture without having to negotiate time off. My monthly Sundays off are respected.

By living in my own house and supporting myself financially I am likely to live in an area longer than a stipendiary priest who may move parishes every seven years or so. NSMs are increasingly seen as 'deployable' and so I am unlikely to serve in the actual parish in which I live. I think that this helped me personally to take on the role of being an ordained minister, and it is useful for parishes that would not otherwise have an assistant priest, but there are drawbacks to this policy. Because I don't live in the parish to which I am licensed I am not involved in its weekday life and so it is hard to feel fully part of it on Sunday.

As a priest who is also in secular employment my relationship with members of the congregation is different from what it would be if I were stipendiary or retired. People know that I have a paid job elsewhere and that I am a volunteer like themselves. If I ask someone to volunteer for something I am not asking them to do something I do not do myself. I often feel that I am not doing as much parish work as I ought, but this is because I experience an expectation that comes from within myself. I have not felt any pressure from either of the parish priests I have worked with to do more than I can comfortably manage.

But for me there is also a negative side to being a non-stipendiary minister. I experienced my call to ministry as a call to being a vicar, that is, a priest in charge of a parish. This was so clear to me that even though I was told that I could only be considered for non-stipendiary ministry because of my age, I felt that I needed to go ahead with the training that was offered to me. I am fortunate in being supported by my husband's earnings and by my part-time employment. When I reach the age of 60 I will be able to claim a pension and I expect to continue working part-time as a counsellor. But it is the prospect of being a permanent curate without authority that alarms me more than the question of whether I am paid a salary by the Church. Learning not to be in charge is a lesson I'm learning, but it's a difficult lesson.

## Balancing roles: work and family responsibilities

Because of my personal circumstances I am fortunate in being able to combine many roles in my life. As a mother of three daughters and a foster daughter of 18 who has lived with us since she was 15, I am glad that I can afford to work part-time and I have always been able to afford to employ someone to help me in the house with cleaning and ironing. My eldest daughter is working and lives locally; the others (aged 18 and 16) will soon be leaving school. Although the girls are all very independent they still require emotional and practical support. My 'day job' as a counsellor in an inner-city girls' school is also intellectually and emotionally demanding and I work two days a week, seeing up to nine girls a day. I would find it very difficult to function in a parish as NSM if I needed to work full-time. However, I am concerned about the extent to which my husband subsidizes the Church by supporting me and I wonder what I would decide to do if that support were withdrawn.

## Balancing roles: creative arts and priesthood

Although I have had various paid careers – science, computing, management and counselling – the one constant in my life has been my need to express myself through creative activity. I work with clay, making both functional pots and figurative sculpture. I also paint and work with textiles. Being an NSM and being in part-time paid employment allows me the freedom to reserve time for going to classes and I hope soon to have a workshop and kiln at home.

In a very busy life I find spiritual nourishment while working with clay. In some way I experience God more fully through the sense of touch than through words or music. The forms that are most beautiful come into existence through being felt, not thought. Art forms a central part of what I can offer as a priest. I have led several sessions entitled 'Clay and Spirituality' with groups of people in Southwark. I want others to experience the joy and inner peace I have come to know through handling clay. Many people believe themselves to be no good at art and I encourage them to have a go and make simple forms. We work in an atmosphere of quiet meditation and people discover for themselves what they are capable of when they allow God to work through their hands. I have also led workshops for church groups, enabling them to make celebratory banners from textile collage and embroidery and to combine this with Bible study.

## Balancing roles: ministry, music, concerts and festivals

I am not musically gifted. I enjoy singing, but I cannot remember tunes. The nearest I come to singing well is my weekly 'Can't Sing Choir' class at Morley College. However, one of my passions is for using music to offer people opportunities for uplifting spiritual experiences. Many people enter a church for the first time to attend a concert and, once there, I hope that they will enjoy not only the music but also the very fact of being in a church building – a place where prayer has been offered to God. Through contacts with singers in my neighbourhood I have been able to arrange some wonderful concerts in my present parish of St Augustine's. The performers have given their time and their talents so that the audience's donations can build up a fund to support arts initiatives at the church, and also to support charity appeals.

I am also actively involved with the annual community festival that has taken place in the community in which I live, Telegraph Hill, every year for the last 11 years. The previous chairperson resigned in order to concentrate on her paid work, so last summer I volunteered to co-ordinate this year's Festival that took place over ten days in March 2005. The Festival is self-financed from ticket sales and the generosity of all the performers and helpers who donate their time and their talents. More than 30 events offer something for everyone. Despite the complexity of co-ordinating a programme of more than 30 events with hundreds of participants and an audience of thousands I had great fun and the Festival was a success. The people who organize the individual events are all experienced, talented and competent and were willing to trust me with the overall co-ordination. During the Festival I was off-duty at St Augustine's and Holy Trinity and was able to accept an invitation to celebrate Holy Communion and to preach at St Catherine's, the parish church of Telegraph Hill. (I also participated in the Festival by exhibiting some of my sculpture in the Open Exhibition.)

I hope to be able to use my experience to help some form of community festival to emerge in Honor Oak using St Augustine's Church as a focal point.

## Balancing roles: a challenge to the Church

Non-stipendiary ordained ministry is a recent development in the Church of England. Most NSMs tend to be licensed as honorary assistant curates although I know of a few exceptions where an NSM is appointed as priest-in-charge. Perhaps the Church could consider the possibilities for greater flexibility in the posts to which ordained clergy are appointed. A mixture of stipends, free housing, expenses, part-time secular employment and pensions from secular employment could support clergy. Without some imaginative thinking about the terms of service offered to NSMs the role may easily become one that is restricted to people who are supported by their partner, are retired, or have no family responsibilities.

It seems to me that the ordination of men and women to be non-stipendiary priests presents an opportunity to the Church that has not yet been fully grasped. The challenge is to find ways to use the skills, enthusiasm and experience of mature people in such a way that they are able to fulfil their vocation. Not all NSMs want to have a position of responsibility in the Church, but there is plenty of potential for using the particular gifts and experience of mature clergy with recent and current experience of secular work. Many are in positions to challenge industry, government and financial institutions with a Christian perspective. They could also offer the Church hierarchy a critique of the Church from the viewpoint of the secular world. The Church has a lot to learn from the assets it possesses in its own clergy.

## Conclusions

I find it difficult to work out where the boundary is between priestly and secular roles, especially in relation to counselling work and in my activities as a community arts organizer. My aim as a priest and counsellor is to be 'congruent', that is, to have all aspects of myself present and working in harmony. I do not stop 'being' a priest even though I may not be 'doing' priestly things. My counselling practice changed when I rediscovered my faith. I do not necessarily speak of my beliefs but the certainty that trust in the love of God can transform suffering helps me to approach each situation with hope and enables me to support and encourage people who are troubled. I do not consciously say or do anything as a counsellor now that I would not have done before ordination, but my theological training has increased the confidence with which I engage with issues of life and death. The experience of having hands laid on me at ordination is something that I carry with me, whether I am in a formal priestly role or in my secular roles.

I have many different roles, in common with many women. It would be easy to feel fragmented with so many identities, but I hope that I have learnt to organize my time so that I have a good balance of different activities. I am grateful to have the opportunity to use my time as I do. I am trying to live my priesthood in all areas of my life, in my secular job, and in my family life and in my artwork, as well as in the parishes to which I am licensed.

In many ways I feel that as an NSM I have remained closer to the laity than I would have done as a stipendiary priest. We have the same concerns about income and housing and time. We are volunteers in a Church that needs us but could sometimes listen to our concerns a little more carefully. We can be missionaries for Christ to the wider world. We can speak the language of the workplace, of schools and the home. To keep my balance I must keep my feet firmly on the ground as I juggle a multitude of balls in the air.

*Further reading*

Fuller, John and Vaughan, Patrick, *Working for the Kingdom: The Story of Ministers in Secular Employment*, SPCK, London, 1986.

# 6. Commissioned to Care
## The Southwark Pastoral Auxiliary

### PETER GRIFFITHS

The righteous will answer him, 'Lord when was it we saw you hungry and gave you food or thirsty and gave you something to drink? And when was it that we saw you a stranger and welcomed you, or naked and gave you clothing? And when was it we saw you sick or in prison, and visited you?' And the king will answer them, 'Truly I tell you, just as you did it to one of the least of these who are members of my family, you did it to me.' (Matthew 25.37–40)

With an interregnum pending, the rector invited me to take communion to a lady who was now homebound but had been used to attending a daily Eucharist. This led on to visiting others, who were either sick, disaffected with the Church or just no longer able to come, but still wanted some contact. The work deepened my knowledge and understanding of the healing ministry in which I was actively involved. I was reasonably confident in what I was doing but I felt that I might do it better if I could receive some training, and I was pleased when my Parochial Church Council (PCC) sponsored me in 1997 to train as a Southwark Pastoral Auxiliary (SPA). A couple of years after being commissioned I was elected by my local colleagues to become Lewisham Archdeaconry SPA and I am in my second and last term of three years in this capacity. On retirement at 65 I applied to become a 'day chaplain' at Southwark Cathedral where twice a month I undertake duties that include being available to talk to anyone seeking pastoral assistance. They might be homeless, jobless, depressed, or receiving treatment at Guy's Hospital: the sort of people to whom Christ ministered, those on the edge or shunned by society. This concept of 'reaching out' lies at the heart of SPA ministry and I hope to show in this chapter that through many different avenues SPAs are well placed to meet those who might be overlooked.

During my training I met Joan. She had recently retired after 30 years as a teacher mainly at Christ Church Primary School in East Greenwich. She was seeking a new challenge and a number of pastoral opportunities had presented themselves in her parish and she responded by offering herself as an SPA. During the training course she joined a group of other trainees on a visit to Brixton Prison. She was so impressed with what she saw there that she asked if she could return for another visit on the following Sunday. This visit confirmed that this was the place where God was leading her and she asked if she could join the chaplaincy team. The chaplains welcomed her warmly and she joined two other SPAs, Linda and Margaret, as part of the inter-faith team that was developing at that time. SPAs working in Brixton Prison were following a tradition that went back to when Jean, one of the chaplains, had begun her ministry there as an SPA in the 1980s. Joan's family and friends were astonished by her decision but she recalls that she had no fear of the prison or the prisoners, who were only too pleased to find someone who could be bothered with them and their situation. She was not concerned with what they had done; but, acknowledging the sparseness of the regime, she offered herself as someone prisoners could talk to and she tried to help them to come to terms with their predicament. Earlier in her life she had had to spend 14 months in a sanatorium, miles from home, suffering the effects of tuberculosis, and this experience helped her to understand what the effects of being in an institution for a long period could be.

SPAs number around 150 throughout the Southwark Diocese and are men and women, commissioned by the diocese, to undertake caring and pastoral work on behalf of the Church in a voluntary capacity. Most SPAs minister within their local churches undertaking such tasks as co-ordinating bereavement support groups, running parent/carer and toddler groups, or organizing pastoral care and visiting teams. Others work in the community within a variety of caring agencies. In some cases their ministry is a combination of the two.

Men represent about 10 per cent of the total number of SPAs and the reason for this is unclear. Some would say that women are instinctive nurturers and tend to have greater capacity for relationship, or that they are more at home with feelings and perhaps better equipped to stand alongside vulnerable people. There could be some truth in this but there's no typical man or typical woman and, while being male or female is not without significance, it doesn't have the imprisoning meaning applied in past times. I believe that in SPA ministry there is a place for different people with different gifts and life experiences, and whether they are men or women, old or young, it is what they can offer individually that is important.

## The beginnings

SPAs have been part of the life of the Southwark Diocese for well over 40 years. They began in the 1960s as a result of a vision that came to Cecilia Goodenough who was the assistant to the diocesan missioner. The country was still living with a half-truth promoted by the prime minister, Harold Macmillan, that 'the people had never had it so good'. Cecilia, a strong and active layperson with a social services background, was greatly aware that there were many who had never had it so bad – the homeless, the poor, prisoners, prisoners' families, and others who were on the edge of society and whose welfare was often ignored by the majority. So a group of laypeople was trained and sent out into the community to serve those who were marginalized in society.

John Nicholson, one of the lay training team in the 1970s recalls that:

for Cecilia, training was mission not method; the uncovering of truth took precedence over the application of technique. Training events for which she was responsible were planned above all with careful attention to ways in which the great sweep of the biblical proclamation might be able to illuminate issues in contemporary society as a clue to the on-going activity of God's self-disclosure. And witnessing to this activity of God was her fundamental understanding of mission.

The early trainees attended lectures on doctrine and ethics and undertook biblical studies in small groups. One such trainee was Molly. She was somewhat startled and severely challenged by the interpretations of the Scriptures put forward by some of her tutors, but she remembers with affection the weekends at the Southwark Diocesan Training Centre, 'Wychcroft', in the heart of the Surrey countryside, where the training was exciting and demanding.

Ruth, who trained in the early 1970s, recalls that a theology for laypeople entitled 'You shall be my people' served as the basis for the weekends. The weekends represented about one third of the course, and the remainder consisted of mid-week lectures and local tutorial groups. She describes the whole training experience as 'a disturbing model of education' that led the participants towards a concept of 'a self-authenticating ministry'. Familiar assumptions about leadership and authority were seriously challenged throughout the training. It was an exciting time for her to be where she was, both spiritually and physically: her faith was deepened, and the training gave her 'a valid sense of the divine'. It was a radical, fraught and political era both in and out of the church and the training was designed to prepare candidates for a difficult task in a complex world.

The strong emphasis on training and working in the community with social outreach led the trainees to a number of community projects, such as Talbot House, a social work settlement, to Local Authority temporary accommodation, such as Chaucer House, which served poor and homeless families, and to the chaplaincies of the Mayday Hospital in Croydon and the Home for Incurables in Wandsworth. Ruth recollects that the young families at Chaucer House were caught up in spirals of deprivation, stress and crime, and she felt challenged to make sense of their common humanity.

Gradually the training moved on to include more work in the parishes. Anne Hoad, another of the lay training team in the 1970s, writes that:

> the search for meaningful community had become more difficult because everyone was inundated with a barrage of information and facts so overwhelming that the world has come to seem an utter bedlam in which people spin, looking for what people have always looked for from the beginning of time – a way of life that has some meaning or sense. The Christian way means a certain degree of order where things have some relationship and can be pieced together into a system that provides some clues to what life is about. This is what SPAs are trained to convey. An SPA starts from where the world is, as it is, not as they would like it to be.

## Today's training course

Training has now become less academic. The emphasis is on presentations followed by discussions in small groups and the whole group together; trainees draw on their own experience of life and share this with each other. This was a new happening for me but I well remember that with the support of those around me and within the confidentiality of the group I gained sufficient confidence to share some painful episodes of my life that I had never discussed openly before.

The present course, drawn up by the Diocesan Co-ordinator of SPA Training, Chris Chapman, and his colleagues begins with trainees building up a profile of their local area. Two modules follow. The first 'God, our ministry and ourselves', focuses on developing skills and awareness that will help trainees to be sensitive to the needs of people in all their diversity and develop self-understanding. The second module, 'God, the Bible and pastoral care', explores how the Bible shapes our vision for pastoral care, and how we use the Bible as a resource for ourselves and others. The module 'Spirituality in life and ministry' reminds everyone that prayer and discipleship are central to everything that we do and aims to strengthen the link between an individual's life with God and the caring work they undertake. The final module, 'Sustaining and developing SPA ministry', focuses on future ministry, with particular emphasis on the agreements needed between SPAs and their parishes and/or agencies and on practical ways of looking after themselves as carers. Ways of recruiting and supporting other volunteers and co-ordinating pastoral care teams are also considered.

In order to gain acquaintance with areas of pastoral care with which they might not be familiar, trainees undertake a series of observation visits to churches or caring agencies. These visits broaden their understanding of pastoral needs and ways of responding. Each trainee undertakes a placement (of approximately 40 hours) in an area of pastoral care previously unknown to them. Here they will be alongside other volunteers and paid workers. At this point a module, 'Caring in Community', looks at practical ways of assessing and responding to pastoral needs in the trainees' neighbourhoods. In small groups, trainees plan presentations on a variety of issues of pastoral concern, focusing in depth on the chosen subjects and developing skills in research, team-working and communication. The finished products are presented at a Project Day for supporters and friends.

The first residential weekend at Wychcroft is a time for getting to know more about each other and one's self. The second residential focuses on 'Ministry in God's diverse world'. Difference, though God-given, is often misinterpreted as a basis for excluding or oppressing people outside our group, so trainees look at God's vision for difference, at how attitudes and structures can value or devalue, include or exclude, and at the connection between difference and power and at practical ways in which individuals, churches or society can work for equal opportunities for all.

A final weekend includes time for prayer, meditation and reflection and a look at the resources available to equip the SPA for ongoing ministry.

The training is designed to enable the trainees to ask questions, to develop skills and abilities, and to discover their own personal gifts for ministry. The training culminates with the commissioning of the SPAs by the bishop in the cathedral to serve on behalf of the diocese by undertaking specific pastoral work in their parishes and/or agencies.

## Supported by the diocese

The diocese's support for SPAs is undertaken by the SPA Council: a body appointed to consider the selection, training and care of all SPAs throughout the Southwark Diocese and for addressing their individual concerns. Archdeaconry SPAs are elected locally to serve for a three-year term, and they are the first point of contact for SPAs who want to share concerns and training and support needs, and they help to ensure that an annual review process takes place. If necessary they may act as a mediator between SPAs, their incumbents or supervisors, and the SPA Council. They call meetings for SPAs in their local area and particularly an annual meeting with their archdeacon. They maintain individual contact with SPAs in their area by whatever means seems appropriate: one-to-one meetings, small group meetings, quiet days and retreats. In the Woolwich Episcopal Area SPAs also have the opportunity to meet with Readers for mutual support.

## Supported by the parish

SPAs undertake work that requires a substantial commitment. Sometimes they have hard and demanding tasks and they can easily become overstretched. Consequently it is important that they are well supported at the local level. The ideal for parish-based SPAs is for them to be part of a local ministry team where clergy, other licensed staff and SPAs can offer each other mutual support and share common concerns. Unlike licensed staff, SPAs have no automatic right to membership of the PCC, but it is good policy for them to be invited to report on their work from time to time and to be given the opportunity to bring any concerns in the wider community to the notice of the PCC. Regular contact with the incumbent is important and not only when passing each other in church or at the time of the annual review. Without adequate support SPAs, like other team members, may soon become demoralized and irritated and their work will suffer accordingly.

## Serving the God who cares

At the beginning of his ministry Christ spoke of his mission by quoting the prophet Isaiah: 'The Spirit of the Lord is upon me, because he has anointed me to bring good news to the poor. He has sent me to proclaim release to the captives and recovery of sight to the blind; to let the oppressed go free, to proclaim the year of the Lord's favour' (Luke 4.8–9). To be able to carry out his ministry of reconciliation, Jesus called 12 others to be with him, to work with him and to learn from him, so that when his own task was finished others empowered by the Holy Spirit would carry on his mission throughout the world. Christ continues to call people today to serve him through a ministry of care. His words, quoted at the beginning of this chapter, set out how we can all serve him by serving one another. A number of SPAs have spoken to me about their work, and their stories are evidence of faithful responses to Jesus' challenge.

*I was hungry and you gave me food, I was thirsty and you gave me something to drink*

Sandy undertook her first 'soup run' seven or eight years ago when she joined a group of people from mixed denominations on a visit to London's homeless. She recalls a mixture of emotions. When all the food and clothes were distributed there was time to stand in the gutter to talk and get to know people. She saw alcohol and drug abuse, and met people with mental health problems and others unable to cope with family break-ups or bereavement. They were vulnerable people, both young and old, living on the streets, while some were staying in hostels or bed and breakfast. She saw caring: a sandwich broken and shared, a cigarette passed around; and she saw people grateful for the little that could be offered to them. She went home that first evening completely exhausted and that night dreamt of hands, all reaching out: some old and gnarled, some soft and clean, male and female, but all reaching out for comfort and love. Then in her dream she saw large, gentle hands that were different from the others. These hands were drying tears and offering a blanket of unconditional love. The hands were scarred and she knew that these were the hands of the crucified Christ. Sandy writes: 'On the soup run my faith is shared without using words. I believe God has placed me among his people who have so little but in return give back so much by way of their vulnerability and trust. I feel humbled to be part of the soup run team.'

I recall some similar feelings on making an observation visit to the Spires Centre in Streatham during my own period of training to be an SPA. The project is supported by the local Anglican and Roman Catholic churches. It provides food and clothing, shower and toilet facilities, healthcare, advice and counselling, and a smile and a cheerful word to many who are homeless or existing below the poverty line. On arrival the place was buzzing and the director told me something of the Centre's aims and objectives and in no time at all asked me if I would like to help out in the clothing store. His sheer enthusiasm for the work rubbed off on me and I became a volunteer for the next three years, one Sunday a month. This was a place where barriers were broken down and as a new-comer I found it hard sometimes to distinguish between who was a centre user, who were staff members, and who were volunteers.

*I was a stranger and you welcomed me, I was naked and you gave me clothing*

Valerie is a retired nurse and when it was suggested that she might become an SPA she thought that it would be a perfect continuation of a life of caring. During the training she undertook a placement at the West Croydon Refugee Centre, and having completed the task she felt that she would like to continue with this work after her commissioning. She was consequently commissioned to her local rural parish and to the Refugee Centre, a complete contrast. She writes:

> Once a week the Centre welcomes as many as one hundred refugees and provides them with a warm place and a hot lunch. We are expected to work in any department, so for my first week I found myself in the kitchen making an apple crumble for a hundred people! I have worked in the crèche, the clothes store, the food store and the household depart-ment. I find that pastoral care is needed for both the refugees and for the many volunteers who give their time so willingly. In spite of being very busy you can always find time to listen. The newly arrived refugee is often frightened and unable to communicate because of language problems (I have become adept at mime); they are lonely and, in winter, very cold. So the priorities are a warm coat, a blanket and a hot meal. Over the years that I have been at the Centre I have found that one thing above all else helps: giving them a big smile and saying 'welcome'. They have probably left their home-land, their possessions and maybe their families behind, and they may be mentally and physically scarred, but, although refugees are not always 'flavour of the month', they are still God's children and are deserving of our love.

*I was sick and you took care of me*

Shirley read an article about SPAs in *The Bridge*, the Southwark diocesan monthly newspaper. It told of the diversity of SPA ministry and she was eager to know more. She felt God calling her and, with the backing of her vicar and PCC, she was accepted for SPA training. She had had a spell in hospital and 'felt called to give something back for the kindness of the hospital chaplain who had given her encouragement and time'. As an SPA Shirley is a member of the chaplaincy team at the Queen Elizabeth Hospital in Woolwich, southeast London, where she spends her Fridays, and on alternate Wednesday afternoons she visits the Bevan Intermediate Care Unit in nearby Thamesmead. She visits patients, takes them communion when requested, listens to their stories, and prays with them. She remembers each of them at the midday prayers in the hospital chapel. She writes: 'This ministry is fulfilling Christ's ministry to the sick and I feel that it is a great privilege to share in this way and to support children, men and women during their stay in hospital.'

Mary is an SPA in a busy south London parish. She was a churchwarden for six years and felt that her spiritual life was being overshadowed by 'too much busyness'. She was certain that this was not what God wanted for her and, after much consideration, prayer and encouragement from her vicar, she went to train as an SPA. Much of her ministry is taken up with visiting people in their homes, some of whom are sick or are housebound for one reason or another. She takes communion to them and spends a lot of time listening. She takes them news of the church and the wider community, and she arranges for them to be brought to some of the outreach events that the parish organizes. She writes:

> I share my love of Christ with others and listen to their problems and needs without being judgemental. I believe that there is good in everyone if you take time to discover it. I know that I can never repay Christ for what he did for me, but by loving my neighbour and by trying my very best to

follow him, by going in whichever direction he leads me, I hope to get it right. I know that God will soon let me know if I don't.

## I was in prison and you visited me

Ann had been a ward sister for many years before her vicar asked her to consider working in the parish as a pastoral assistant caring for the elderly. During her training as an SPA she paid a visit to Brixton Prison. She met the chaplains and learnt of the need for volunteers who were prepared to come in and help in the pastoral care of the prisoners and the staff. In addition to her parish role, Ann was commissioned to work at the prison. She found that the men had a great need to be able to talk confidentially to a sympathetic listener. Listening to and praying with prisoners has become a most important part of her ministry. It enables her to show something of Christ's love to some who have never known love. The chaplaincy provides church services, Bible study groups and an Alpha Course. Ann writes:

> Every time I visit the prison I do not know what I will be involved with but knowing that our Lord is with me I find that the Holy Spirit enables me to speak words of compassion and comfort to the men. I see my ministry as helping the men to see that through the love of Christ they may better come to terms with their situation and be better equipped for life on the outside.

Claudette was asked to take a different role within the world of law and order when she was invited to undertake the role of police chaplain. She believes that her known Christian commitment and her professional role as a health visitor, where listening skills are a very important aspect of the job, were important considerations when she was put forward for this new role. She has been a police chaplain for the past five years. On a regular basis she visits the local station, where she is known to 'loiter with intent'. She meets with uniformed and non-uniformed members of the force, and 'confidentiality' is her watchword. She remembers some words of the Revd Francis Pole, who was once co-ordinator of police chaplaincy in the diocese: 'Police chaplains are there to be a friend, confidante and occasionally to be an advocate. Their role is unique in that it has a distinct spiritual identification.'[1]

## Acting out the New Commandment

SPAs, in seeking to serve the God who cares, look to Christ who, loving the human race, joined it and suffered for it. They seek to follow Christ's commandment 'to love one another as I have loved you' and in doing so endeavour to become more real, more human. This is Good News: this is the gospel in *action*.

### Note

1 Pole, Francis, *Handbook for Police Chaplains*, Metropolitan Police, London, 2000.

# 7. Here to Stay
## The Ordained Local Minister

### ARTHUR OBIORA

You then, my child, be strong in the grace that is in Christ Jesus; and what you have heard from me through many witnesses entrust to faithful people who will be able to teach others as well. (2 Timothy 2.1, 2)

## Selection

Ordained Local Ministry is shared ministry. The first I heard about it was at a Parochial Church Council meeting in my parish of St Catherine, Hatcham, on Telegraph Hill at New Cross in south London. A new training scheme was about to start, and we were being asked whether we wanted the parish to be considered. If so, who was our candidate to be?

We invited the Revd Geoff Mason to a meeting. He explained that only parishes in which there was already shared ministry would be considered, and that candidates for ordination had to be long-standing members of their community and had to intend to remain there. I was already a Reader, I had been churchwarden and covenant secretary, I had been in the parish for 30 years, and I did indeed intend to stay. I also knew that having a young family meant that I couldn't train full-time to be a priest, so this course looked the right way to go.

The process started. I had to see the Director of Ordinands and the Examining Chaplain, who asked me questions about my background and my faith: and then I had to go to a selection conference at Maryvale, a retreat house in a most beautiful setting. All of us on the conference were candidates for Ordained Local Ministry, and we were nervous. We thought that the selectors were a bit tense, too: first of all because they weren't quite sure what they were looking for, and second because one of the selector's wives was ill. One candidate in particular did a lot of pacing up and down; and one of the candidates, Hazel Kimber, described the event as 'challenging, nerve-racking and faith-testing; encouraging and deflating and at times emotionally draining'. I agree. We were extensively questioned on our backgrounds, our involvement in the Church, involvement in the community, faith, prayer, worship, and educational attainments. (Although we were told that lack of educational attainment was no bar to being a candidate, a certain level of literacy was clearly required to cope with the course.) There were role-plays and groupwork.

There were ten candidates at the conference, and eight of us were selected for training. (The other two were later selected for Non-stipendiary Ministry.)

## Training

The training was very practical. The first task was a parish audit, or neighbourhood profile, which we had to work on with a group from the parish. St Catherine's had recently had a parish audit, so some of the work had been done already, but there was still much to be done, and I learnt a lot about the housing tenures in the parish, and explored parts of the parish that I didn't know so well. Working on the profile with the group from the parish who were going to accompany me through the training was an important bonding experience.

There were placements. The parish placement was at St James's, Bermondsey. The liturgy at St Catherine's is quite catholic, and the Eucharist is at the heart of the parish's life.

St James's is much more evangelical, and initially I found it hard to identify with their way of worship. It was a learning experience, and I was more used to it by the second week and quite at home by the fifth.

It was the placement at the youth club at the Telegraph Hill Centre, next to St Catherine's, which was the most powerful learning experience. I had never done any youth work, except for bringing up our own two children, and here I was expected to relate to teenagers with attitudes very different from those of our Sinclair and Konrad. A particularly fulfilling part of the task was the work with young people with disabilities; but coping with groups of teenagers hanging round the coffee bar which I was trying to run was more challenging.

The placement at Lewisham Hospital was deeply moving. I would spend the evenings on the ward, at the intensive therapy unit, on the children's wards, and in the special care baby unit – marvelling that such tiny babies could survive. The mortuary was a bit of a shock, as I hadn't seen bodies in drawers in large fridges before. I worked with the porters, listened to the pressures the nurses were under, and heard the doctors speak about their problems. The whole experience prepared me for the kind of compassionate listening a priest has to do. And I learnt to pray with people, to bring people to faith in God, and to help people to explore the faith they'd got.

As well as the placements there were weekends at Wychcroft, the diocesan training centre, where we learnt the practical things a priest needs to know, such as preaching, voice control, bereavement counselling, and the like.

One evening a week we met together as a group with the Revd Stephen Lyon, the course's Principal, and the Revd Judith Roberts, the Vice Principal, and often with a visiting teacher, to study the Old and New Testaments, liturgy, ethics, Church history and pastoral care.

An important part of the preparation for Ordained Local Ministry is having a personal tutor. Fr Graham Preston fulfilled this role, and after the course was over he became my spiritual director. We meet as necessary, we pray, and we discuss issues facing our ministry.

The ordination to the diaconate was a deeply moving experience for me, and I think for the parish. My ordination as a priest a year later was perhaps an even more important event for me and for the parish, and that evening I concelebrated at the Eucharist with Alison Tyler, who had been ordained a non-stipendiary priest the same day.

## Being an Ordained Local Minister

Telegraph Hill is now even more multicultural than it was when we prepared the neighbourhood profile. It is easy to get to New Cross from Central London late at night, so we have lots of musicians and actors; and the large basements of the houses encourage artists, potters and sculptors. It's a friendly place, with small shops (though not as many as there were before Sainsburys was built). Until our dog Basil died recently at the ripe old age of 14 I walked Telegraph Hill Park with him every morning. This was a crucial part of my relationship with the community, as it was where conversations happened.

People talk to me: this is a vital part of my ministry. People in the parish talk to me, friends of people I know in the parish talk to me, and ask for advice, prayer, and information about the Christian Faith. It's because I'm a priest and they know that I belong here that they talk to me. The teenagers I got to know at the youth club are now adults and they are parents, and they talk to me – and I recently baptized one of their children. A particularly important time for me was a visitation I conducted, visiting lots of people in the congregation and outside it to talk to them about God, and from this have come requests for further visits.

I receive from the people who talk to me at least as much I give to them. This was particularly the case recently when I ministered to an elderly lady until she died. Her strong faith strengthened mine.

At the heart of my ministry is the Eucharist. I share the presiding with our vicar, Canon Francis Makambwe, and I take communion to the elderly and the sick so that they can remain members of the congregation.

On Saturdays at 4 p.m. there is a Bible study. The numbers go up and down, but I stick with it because it matters. People bring their questions and we discuss them.

And occasionally I still go to the youth club.

This is very much a *shared* ministry. First of all it is shared with the incumbent. We both preside at the Eucharist, lead Evening Prayer, conduct weddings and funerals, visit the sick, baptize infants, and prepare adult candidates for baptism and confirmation.

The group that accompanied me through my training no longer meets, but I receive plenty of support through the staff meeting (Canon Makambwe, our Reader Lesley Goodwin, a retired priest, the Revd James Bogle, and myself), and also through the PCC. Some long-standing friends who accompanied me through my training are still a support: Jeremy Palmer, Ann Atkins, Pearletta Williams, Maud Foreman and Dennis Bryant. And now there is someone else thinking about Ordained Local Ministry and someone else training to be a Reader, and we shall support them. The parish has a strong tradition of encouraging people to discover their gifts and use them – and I now have sufficient experience of this happening to be able to help to select people for training as Southwark Pastoral Auxiliaries.

## Local?

What does 'local' mean? My licence is to St Catherine's, Hatcham, and that's where I preside at the Eucharist, lead Bible studies, and visit people. But 'local' for me is also the Department of Work and Pensions office where I work. People there know that I am a priest so they come to talk to me, just as people do in the parish. I attend the Bible study group there (which others run) and we discuss how to interpret the Bible.

The way we live today, each of us might have one, two or more 'local's, and in all of them we exercise our ministry. We have a responsibility to do so.

## Shared ministry?

Shared ministry is about:

- every Christian being called to share God's ministry in the world, at home, in the workplace, in the community and the Church;
- the way each congregation seeks to organize its corporate life and work for God's purpose and mission;
- how we seek to enable a variety of gifts of leadership in the Church – pastoral care, teaching the gospel and visiting;
- a way of life rather than a structure, liberating the gifts of all the baptized for the service of Christ;
- sharing the responsibilities of the Church by all, clergy and laity;
- sharing the pains of others – bereavement and when there is illness in a family;
- looking after young children in need, the elderly or people with special needs.

The parish's shared ministry really comes into its own when the vicar leaves, as happened soon after my ordination. I received lots of support from the churchwardens, others in the congregation, and neighbouring clergy. And ministry was well shared when our new vicar had to go into hospital.

## The future?

The training scheme for Ordained Local Ministry is both practical and appropriately academic, and it prepared us well to be priests in our parishes. The course is now validated by Bangor University, and candidates receive a diploma when they finish it. The course is still practical, and I hope that it will remain so, as its task is to train people to be priests in their parishes.

## Conclusion

An important concern for Ordained Local Ministry candidates is whether people will regard them as second-class priests. That hasn't been my experience. In the parish, both Francis Makambwe and myself are priests.

I have been asked on many occasions what it felt like as an OLM to be in one place for so long and remain fresh? The simple answer is the love I have for St Catherine's and the people. Some unfortunately have died but with new members following behind them the tradition left by those who have gone is still strong. To sustain me, I am fortunate to have in the parish people whose love, honesty and discipleship are in concert with mine. With the help of the Holy Spirit, these people have helped me to keep going.

### Further reading

Torry, Malcolm and Heskins, Jeffrey (eds), *Ordained Local Ministry: A new shape for ministry in the Church of England*, Canterbury Press, London, 2006.

# 8. Professionals between the Church and the World

## Licensed Lay Workers

### GILLIAN REEVE

To each is given the manifestation of the Spirit for the common good. (1 Corinthians 12.5–7)

## Who are we talking about?

Even a cursory glance at the current Southwark Diocesan Directory shows that there is now only a handful of Licensed Lay Workers (LLWs) in the diocese. Thirty years ago it was very different. This chapter looks at some of the reasons for this change and poses the question as to whether there are forms of lay ministry that should be formally recognized in one way or another.

## My own history

I came into accredited lay ministry more by accident than design. In 1968, after having worked for several years with the Inter-Church Aid Department of the World Council of Churches in Geneva, I started a social work training course that lasted for two and a half years at the Josephine Butler College in Liverpool. This was an Anglican foundation and the training there resulted in a social work diploma as well as the 'Inter-Diocesan Certificate' (IDC). The IDC meant that I could be licensed to be involved in a parish as well as undertake a professional role in that place. My social work training (particularly through the practical placements I had undertaken), enabled me to qualify as a youth worker and, in 1970, I was appointed in this capacity to a parish on the northern outskirts of Liverpool, licensed by the Bishop of Liverpool.

This was one of those near impossible situations of the late 1960s and early 1970s. The parish was made up of some good 1930s private housing on one side of the main road out of Liverpool into Lancashire, a mid-1930s quite well established council estate, and some very new sprawling docklands overspill. The wind-lashed new estate petered out into damp fields while the buses were always full with people returning to Liverpool for work, school, shops and family. The church was part of the new build and next to it was a new youth centre, purpose-built in a style replicated in so many areas of new housing estates across Liverpool and other parts of the country as local authorities attempted to meet the needs of young people (needs well documented in the Albemarle Report[1]).

The strength of being seen to be part of the church staff, as well as having a professional role in my own right, made it possible to forge links with a wider range of people and agencies than I think might have been the case had I been just a youth worker or just a parish worker. I was also given a wide range of opportunities liturgically, and it was as natural to be sitting each week listening to Evensong with an elderly lady as it was to be going canoeing with a group of young people on the nearby canal (in our own-made canoes) or to be liaising with the Housing Development Manager on the estate who happened to be an ex Roman Catholic priest. These situations and the Church's liturgy belonged together.

This was the model that I therefore had when I came to work as warden to the Telegraph Hill Centre at St Catherine's, New Cross, in 1972, just as it was being opened. I was employed by the Telegraph Hill Neighbourhood Council, then with a staff team of about 12 people. These included community workers, youth workers, and staff for the new Centre, where one of the churchwardens was appointed as Centre caretaker. The parish staff consisted of the incumbent, Canon Allan Auckland, a curate, a woman parish worker and an honorary curate, the Revd Malcolm Johnson (described at that time in the diocesan directory as a priest-worker, and employed as the director of the Telegraph Hill Neighbourhood Council) and myself. I was commissioned by the Bishop of Southwark and received his licence to preach.

This was a time of great hope for the parish and the community. An enormous amount of time, money and energy had gone into the building of the Centre and while some people had been devastated at how much of the actual church building had gone into the forming of the Centre, many more had been very supportive and worked hard on the project. But there were also concerns both that the Centre might become dominated by the church, and that it would become a white elephant at the top of the hill when the real work of the Neighbourhood Council should be 'out there' in the community. These tensions were to be experienced in many ways and there was an enormous value in at least some of us having both a professional role and an accepted place within the liturgical setting. It was impossible totally to separate the two. I always felt accepted as a full member of the parish church and of the parish's staff team, all of us having roles that, although different, might overlap at times. It was impossible not to bring situations from the Centre and our work in the community into sermons and other parts of the liturgy, even though there might be the odd skirmish or two from a zealous churchwarden as to what it was appropriate for a woman to be doing as part of the liturgy.

There were also other tensions arising in the community where the dual role was helpful. Particularly through Malcolm Johnson's work with Sybil Phoenix, then leader of the Moonshot Youth Club in Deptford and a Methodist local preacher, the community became aware of the number of Afro-Caribbean families who were concerned about their children's education. Over the years this work, shared by both the Centre and the church, became part of the strength of the neighbourhood and has set solid foundations for the way St Catherine's continues to work.

When I left Telegraph Hill Centre in 1977 I did so to work as a social worker with Bromley Welcare and received a licence from the Bishop of Rochester; but I continued to live at New Cross and to be a member of St Catherine's, and ever since then I have felt included in the staff team.

## A different perspective

Working in Bromley my status as a licensed worker was different because I did not relate to any particular parish; rather, it was part of my role to represent Welcare to all the parishes that supported its work financially and in other ways. I was with Bromley Welcare until 1984, by which time the world and the Church were changing. I was more conscious that I was straddling *different* worlds, some with considerable wealth and some containing poverty, hurt, loneliness, struggle and despair. I wanted to connect them. So when I was invited to congregations or church groups to talk about the work of Welcare and to persuade them to continue their financial support, I put the work in human terms, for people are not just numbers or victims. Over the years we developed some of the work so that we could engage with families in different ways, for instance, by running holiday play schemes, after school activities, and holidays away. In this way the churches could be involved through using their skills and expertise and not just through their financial support. So the relationship became less one of benevolence and more one of active participation. This was perhaps particularly important as the years went by and the 1980s became the age of individualism and consumerism.

## Moving onwards

Since 1989 I have worked at the Copleston Centre Church in Peckham as its co-ordinator. This has been another different experience. I was appointed by the management committee and again it seemed to come as rather a surprise that they had employed someone who had a connection with a local church.

This was a new post made possible by one of the first Church Urban Fund (CUF) grants made in the Diocese of Southwark. However, the relationship between the incumbent and the co-ordinator had not been addressed. Although I was not technically part of the church as an organization (it is an Anglican/United Reformed Church Partnership so it includes both Anglican and URC ways of working) it seemed to be tacitly understood that we operated within the same ethos even when we differed over ways of doing things. I did not feel that I was expected to be part of the regular worshipping community as it was acknowledged that I was involved elsewhere; but it was important to be at certain events in order to work alongside the congregation as much as possible and to be able to explore ways of working together within the overall vision for the Centre and the church.

## An historical overview

Over the last 30 years events in the Church and the world around us have affected considerably the way women's ministry and lay ministry have been perceived. In the late 1960s lay ministry virtually equated with women's ministry. In the Southwark Diocesan Directory for 1974, for example, there is a list of 44 women described as 'deaconesses and women workers' who held the bishop's licence. There were also 19 women who held the 'Bishop's Authority' and 22 listed as Southwark Pastoral Auxiliaries. Thirty years later there were no deaconesses listed, three licensed lay workers and over 140 SPAs. The overwhelming difference between the two directories is, of course, the very considerable number of ordained women now working in parishes or chaplaincies within the diocese and also a number of male SPAs. Thirty years ago over half of the women listed held the bishop's licence primarily in relation to the post for which they were employed rather than being appointed as a worker to a specific parish. The places where they were trained have now largely disappeared: Greyladies in Blackheath, Dalton House in Bristol, Gilmore House. The College of the Ascension, where the Cambridge Certificate of Theology could be gained, still remains, but it now has a very different focus. Included in the list in the 1974 Directory are some women who made a very significant contribution to the life of the Church in Southwark during the 1970s and 1980s: Margaret Turk, Gwen Rymer and Eileen Edgar.

In 1984 a report to the Candidates Committee of the Advisory Council for the Church's Ministry (ACCM) expressed some concern that the work of redefining the role of accredited lay workers was being postponed until the question of deaconesses becoming deacons had been resolved. It was noted that the 'accredited lay ministry historically had been an alternative model, primary for women's ministry, from that of the Deaconess order'.

The report continues:

A full-time accredited lay ministry allows for a number of other competent and qualified workers in the Church to remain within the Laos (the laity, the people of the Church) and penetrate aspects of human society that may best be served by identification with, rather than separately from, those being ministered to. Some lay men and women may still be needed to continue to be freed to do this work in order to offer a full-time commitment in a variety of human zones where the ordained person is less likely to gain an entry. This could be of immense value in the work of industrial mission, youth and community, social and educational services sponsored by the Church.[2]

The report also posed the question as to whether 'the changing social agency environment and rise of the Welfare State [has] led to some demise of church social work and some increase in the desire to be a clergyperson instead'. This clearly is a significant point. In the 1980s the ordination of women was becoming a serious issue. In 1987 the order of deacons was opened to women and most deaconesses and some lay workers were ordained. In 1992 the vote in Synod opened ordination as priests to women.

This was also a time when some of us who had worked as lay workers for several, and often for many, years, felt confused, or that their ministry was being questioned and undervalued. When talking recently to one of the now fairly elderly ladies in the current Directory, she said to me, 'Don't ask me what I did, as I did everything'. For many, this was how it was, and no other form of accreditation was felt to be necessary.

Others of us who have not sought ordination have not necessarily not done so on the grounds of age or of the feeling that they wouldn't have us anyway, but more from the feeling that it would be almost a betrayal of the kind of ministry we have exercised over many years. We have worked alongside other lay- and clergypersons to offer as complete a form of ministry as possible. None of us, I am sure, would want to detract from the struggle of those women who have sought ordination, but many of us would claim, here in the diocese of Southwark, that we have been able to exercise a true and valid vocation within whatever profession we have chosen to follow.

A paper written in 1993 by Caroline Barker-Bennett[3] outlined this tension. In the early 1970s Caroline had left teaching to become a youth worker in the diocese. Much of her work was funded by the local authority. She undertook theological training, became a Reader, and gained experience of pastoral ministry. From there she went on to become an industrial chaplain in the Diocese of Newcastle, and then Director of Education in Manchester diocese, and she has recently retired from being Director of Education in Bristol diocese. In her article she wrote:

My question to the Church is, 'Are you going to understand and value what I feel called to do?' Now that women will be able to be ordained it is much more difficult to explain my position. It would, I feel, have been harder for me now to have been taken on as a lay industrial chaplain than when women could not be ordained.

She suggests that the Church of England's preoccupation with the ordination of women has pushed the Church into a 'preoccupation with clericalization, e.g. more and more kinds of ordained ministry have been created: NSMs, Ministers in Secular Employment, Ordained Local Ministry, so that it is very hard to escape ordination if you have a sense of vocation at all.'

## Where is accredited lay work now?

In 1997 the Diaconal Association of the Church of England (DACE) produced a publicity leaflet. It described Accredited Lay Work (ALW) as a:

nationally accredited ministry of the Church of England (that) is regarded as one of the Diaconal Ministries. ALWs are people who are called to a professional ministry in the Church of England, yet do not feel God is calling them to be ordained. They value their lay status, and wish to work alongside people, as Christ walked with his friends on the road to Emmaus, and seek to undergird their work with theological training. They can be a bridge between fellow [sic.] laity and clergy.[4]

In the Diocese of Southwark there are quite a lot of people employed by social projects either attached to or sponsored by churches and often partly funded in their initial stages through the Church Urban Fund (CUF). Should they be accredited in any way? CUF came into being as a result of the *Faith in the City* report,[5] and since 1989 a considerable number of churches or deaneries have received funding to address issues of social concern. There is even a loose network of workers involved in such projects, but a worker's relationship to the parish or deanery is often complex or unclear. The question has to be asked: what difference would it make to both the project and the parish if the relationship were to be made more explicit and for there to be a clearer expectation of the mutual role between the worker and the parish as well as between the project and the parish? On the other hand, in these days when backgrounds are more diverse than they were 25 years ago, it could well be that the most appropriately qualified person for the post would not wish to make such a commitment to the worshipping community. Even church staff and project staff sharing staff meeting agendas and policies is not always the norm.

Both the Church and the world seem to be very different places from when I, virtually accidentally, became involved in an accredited lay ministry. The value for me at that time, and for others with whom I have spoken, was that the Church was prepared to recognize the professional work that was being undertaken in its name and was prepared to pay for it, or at least to take some responsibility to see that it was funded. The fact that most of the people involved 25 to 30 years ago were women is also significant. It gave them an authority and credibility that counted when, on the whole, women did not have the same profile as today.

There is a steady increase in the number of people coming forward for SPA training. This is a significant non-stipendiary ministry. And in other dioceses, as I have discovered by being able to attend the national Local Ministry Conference during the past couple of years, there are quite elaborate training programmes for preparing ministry teams containing both lay and ordained people. Generally, however, the only stipendiary person will be the incumbent. The only exception I know of is in the Diocese of Lincoln where in the 1980s a lay minister was appointed to lead a team running a parish.

I hope that this chapter will have raised some of the issues which our Church needs to address in order that we can value and cherish equally a range of ministries containing both women and men and both lay and ordained. A particular question we might wish to consider further is this: Where someone has been professionally trained as a community development or social worker, or as a youth worker, or in some other such capacity, and where they work in a church-related project, and where they, the project and the parish believe that a structural relationship between the parish and the worker would benefit the relationship between the parish and the project, then maybe the bishop should licence that worker to the parish, thus giving them a place in the parish's staff team and a role in the Church's liturgy.

Maybe Licensed Lay Workers have a future.

## Notes

1 *The Youth Service in England and Wales* (The Albermarle Report), Ministry of Education, UK, 1960.

2 Rymer, Gwen, *Report of the Candidates Committee of the Advisory Council for the Church's Ministry*, Advisory Committee for the Church's Ministry, London, 1984.

3 Barker-Bennett, Caroline, 'How to escape ordination: the lay vocation', unpublished paper, 1993.

4 *Accredited Lay Workers in the Church of England*, The Diaconal Association of the Church of England, Chatham, 1997.

5 *Faith in the City: The Report of the Archbishop of Canterbury's Commission on Urban Priority Areas*, Church House Publishing, London, 1985.

# 9. The Ministry of Music
## The Parish Musician

CYNTHIA FINNERTY

Happy are the people who worship you with songs. (Psalm 89.15)

## Labour and make music

My earliest memories of church are connected with the music, and in particular choruses sung at Mothers' Union meetings that I attended with my mother. If I was good I was allowed to choose one, usually 'PPY' (I'm H.A.P.P.Y.). Later I struggled to pick out the notes of my favourites on the piano. I would probably have given up the rather boring piano lessons and the restrictions of practice time if I did not have the goal of being able to play these songs. The hymnbook was more often on the piano than books of scales and studies. My secondary school had as a motto 'Labour and Make Music', and I remember thinking what a strange statement, but I now know exactly what it means.

It was partly through the repetition of hymns and choruses that I came to Christian faith and felt able to demonstrate and share that faith. The enveloping sound of organ music, both playing and listening, creates in me a readiness to pray and worship: a coming closer to God. I soon became involved in playing at my family's church and began to labour and make music. For me the music became a way of expressing myself non-verbally and I think that for many people a piece of music may speak more than words: it is an effective form of communication and has the power to evoke a variety of human emotions and to create the right atmosphere. The words of liturgy are an important part of our worship, but for some of us their importance is enhanced by music. I began to explore the musical aspect of worship and gradually to take on a new role, which is perhaps best described in a phrase used in America – 'minister of music'.

## Ministry of music

I was asked to write this chapter wearing my parish musician's hat – or should it be gown? I was still at school when I took on my first role as organist. As well as the usual services – three most Sundays – I was expected to conduct choir practices, and sort out junior choir training and pay the choristers, but I had little or no say in the choice of hymns or settings. I did what I was told. Weddings in those days were also an enormous commitment. One memorable Saturday we managed to fit in five. The choir was delighted with the financial gain, but to get rid of excess energy we made them run round the block while photos were being taken and bribed them with ice creams. It was a hot day.

To fit in time at the organ I would trot from my school at lunchtime and eat my sandwich while practising pedals. I was very aware of my own limitations and inexperience and was grateful for the understanding and encouragement given to me by clergy, choir and congregation.

After three years' teacher training I came to St George's, Westcombe Park, as a temporary replacement for their organist who had gone to university. The weeks turned to months and I so enjoyed the worship, fellowship and support that I'm still there, more than 30 years later. My role gradually developed from organist to parish musician as my commitment and involvement with the parish increased: discussions with clergy, planning services, convening a worship committee, and attending Parochial Church Council (PCC) meetings: the ministry of music.

## Music in the parish

Every parish is unique, with its own traditions and resources. In our area we have cathedral-standard music, traditional-style choir and organist, music group with worship songs, and a variety of other genres, including St George's where it may be straightforward hymn accompaniment, or an orchestra from the junior church and young people, or a recorder group, or occasionally an augmented choir to tackle something like Stainer's *Crucifixion*. I inherited a robed men and boys choir in the 1960s. Ladies were permitted when altos were needed for a choral work, but considerable discussion went on before I was allowed to audition girls for the choir. When I started, choristers had time to practise – twice a week in fact – until homework set in when they went to secondary school. Now even primary-age children seem to be restricted. After one particular recruitment drive involving local schools when church members had failed to fill the choir pews, I was congratulating myself on the successful outcome when it became apparent that they all punctually attended the Wednesday rehearsal, which included music tuition as well as singing, and then did not attend Sunday services. Enquiries revealed that the family weekend away was the reason. I needed subtle ploys to persuade parents that Sunday worship was part of the deal. Parents were invited to come into church to listen to their children singing at the end of a Wednesday session. They were so good, wouldn't it be nice if they could perform at the Harvest Festival? Parents were welcome to come, and to bring family and friends. We met with some support, and a few parents actually began to attend services, making the choir an evangelism outreach opportunity.

That worked that time, but things change, and Sunday sports fixtures now compete with church attendance. Some parishes still manage to keep regular choirs running, but not at St George's at the moment. Which doesn't mean that there's no music. There are more people involved than ever.

## Music in worship

The first question to ask is about the role of music in worship. The Archbishops' Commission on Church Music published *In Tune with Heaven* in 1992. This analysed in depth the enormous wealth and diversity of music within the Church of England. Its summary of the response to the question 'What is the role of music in worship?' was:

- to worship and praise God
- to uplift the soul
- to promote corporate awareness and fellowship.

Which, if any, of these statements would your parish identify with? And who is it referring to? The musician? The choir? Or dare I suggest everyone?

Surely everyone should be included, and the parish needs to ensure that the music is accessible, inclusive, and relevant for all worshippers. On an activity day at St George's in preparation for Pentecost everyone who was there took part in a creative improvisation on the theme of the Spirit using simple percussion and tuned instruments.

Having established within the parish a definition of the role of music, a careful investigation and extensive identification of all the musical resources available needs to be carried out: but by whom? At this point the question of who is responsible for the music arises.

Parishes often give the overall responsibility to the parish musician, but the Church's Canon Law states that the minister is responsible for the performance of divine service.

> Where there is an organist, choirmaster or director of music the minister shall pay due heed to his advice and assistance in the choosing of chants, hymns, anthems, and other settings, and in the ordering of the music of the church; but at all times the final responsibility and decision in these matters rests with the minister. (Canon B20)

So it is understandable that conflict might develop between ministers and musicians unless careful structures are in place and regular communication links exist. At meetings of my local organists' association conversations usually begin with 'Are you still at St Blogg's?' So often the answer is 'No', and an outpouring of the divorce follows. However, this is not always the case, and in my own situation the 4 weeks' engagement became a 30-year commitment. It has not been without its moments. For example, 48 hours before being televised live I was still trying to get details so that the choir and I could rehearse. No one seemed to listen to my worries about pitch for the singers outside the building processing in to the first hymn to join me and the congregation. Another time I arrived at church to be told: 'O, by the way, there is a film crew coming.' In general, though, through a good working understanding and a flexible approach, few of these problems occur and we are happy.

It is important that a parish continuously evaluates and assesses its own situation. Changes are often necessary, but they need to be carefully thought out and shared with those involved. I rapidly found out that introducing a small group of musicians with PCC approval upset Daisy. After that I always found an opportunity to talk to her before something unusual was to happen, and then Daisy was happy. She just did not like surprises. Some worshippers welcome variety, others prefer tradition, and keeping everyone happy is a challenge for worship leaders and musicians.

## Parish musician

Parishes where the relationship between musician and parish is happy are firmly built on good understanding and honest communication. Job descriptions for parish musicians are usually brief and only include the tip of the iceberg. Just take a look in the *Church Times*:

. . . develop a small choir and music group
. . . A committed Christian with a passion for worship in a
variety of music styles

. . . an accomplished and creative musician to help us enrich
our liturgy

. . . opportunity to build on quality tradition.

There is a real need for the parish to draw up a clear job description as a starting point for initial discussions and a basis for a
formal written agreement between parish and musician. Then
– maybe – a harmonious team will develop.

With so few musicians available and willing, parishes often
persuade and pressurize people to take on roles for which they
do not have adequate musicianship and experience. Musician
and parish need to be open with each other, and realistic targets need to be set. It may be necessary for the parish to invest
in training for their musician or to support them by providing
expertise in areas that are not within their experience. A good
musician may not have administrative skills, and these could
be provided by a parish administrator. A good accompanist
may not be able to keep a lively junior choir under control
but would survive with the support of other adults. Many
musicians are busy people and need support with such tasks
as keeping music tidy; and just whose responsibility *is* the
upkeep of the choir robes? Someone volunteering to make sure
enough copies of music are available, including large copies
for the people who forget their glasses, is really helpful.

## Time for music

For a parish musician it is not just a case of turning up for the
service on Sunday. Time spent varies enormously. One colleague allocates one day a month and one morning each week,
and that does not include personal practice time. Another
plans with worship leaders one evening a month; others talk
about the time spent in communication on telephones and e-
mails. Rehearsal times depend on the number of choirs and
music groups. One parish musician distributes music to players two weeks in advance and then rehearses for an hour before
the service; another has to direct three choir practises each

week. In my parish, which does not regularly have a choir, rehearsals are held when necessary for a special occasion such as Christmas, Easter or a Confirmation service, and finding a convenient time for everyone is a nightmare. Our junior musicians rehearse after the morning service, and at the same time recorder lessons are given by another member of the parish. Time spent sharing skills and encouraging others to take over the recorder group or conduct the orchestra helps towards a collaborative approach to parish music so that music becomes teamwork: a shared ministry.

## Choice of music

Considerable time is also needed for planning and choosing music. This is often a point of contention, and communication between musician and worship leaders and between parish musician, choir and players must be established. This all takes time, so planning needs to start early. While rehearsals for Christmas are still happening Easter needs to be planned. Parish musicians have to be looking forward, and an understanding of this by the parish is essential. Twenty-four hours or less notice of the inclusion of a new worship song can be very stressful. Finances also come into the equation – can the parish afford new music? And it is the musician's responsibility to make sure that any copyright rules are obeyed.

Can you keep everyone happy? No, of course not – but remembering that you are part of a team creating an act of worship is critical; knowing the liturgical setting and the ambiance of the occasion is essential; and being aware of the resources available and the type of participants at the act of worship is necessary before attempting to select the music. The willingness and ability to work collaboratively will help to create the required happy outcome.

Weddings need considerable care. Auntie Flo will never forgive you if you play the wrong tune to 'All things bright and beautiful', and I need several weeks' notice for challenging pieces like Widor's *Toccata*. Communications concerning the happy couple's musical requirements should not be left to the minister unless s/he is musically literate.

Funerals can cause problems for the musician as there is often little notice to find the deceased's favourite hymn from 19--? The parish do not seem to understand why I keep so many old hymnbooks, but *Golden Bells* – remember it anyone? – has often come to my rescue. Trying to read the music for 'Jerusalem' through tears when the funeral is for a much-loved member of the congregation is really hard.

## Communication

One of the most essential skills of a parish musician is the ability to communicate, not just musically, but in many different ways. Discussions with the minister and worship leaders, persuading the junior choir parents to support extra rehearsals for Christmas, conducting choir and orchestra, even, ever so gently, telling Maud that she is no longer able to reach top A and that G# won't do, or convincing the PCC that they need to spend £xxxxx on the organ – these are all part of the job. If communications lapse, especially with the minister who, by canon law, is responsible for the music, then it will probably lead to a break-up – or a walk-out.

Time spent listening to exactly what a worship leader is trying to express in terms of musical contributions for an innovative service of healing can result in benefits to the act of worship and can lessen the likelihood of disputes. Of course it has to be a two-way exchange, and perhaps the leader also needs to listen to the musician.

## Training

Music in a parish should not be static. The parish musician should be monitoring, assessing and evaluating (and yes, I am a teacher), listening constructively to comments after a service, and communicating findings back to the parish when appropriate. Very often a chance remark sparks off an initiative: a young person's comment about music being 'old people stuff' resulted in a challenge to do something themselves. They did, and a production of a show called 'George' involving people of all ages was performed in our church.

The parish musician needs to make decisions about when and how often rehearsals occur (not forgetting child protection issues with junior choristers), and about when it is necessary to hold a recruitment drive.

Training choirs and music groups goes with the job and there are many instruction books: but what about teaching the congregation? Introducing new songs, hymns and settings without provoking an immediate negative reaction takes ingenuity of the highest degree, particularly when you have no choir to introduce them. I sneak unfamiliar hymn tunes into voluntaries weeks before we sing the hymn, plan activity days that include teaching new settings, and get the junior church to learn and perform a new song. I have tried the 'before the service rehearsal', but this does not work particularly well in my situation when most of the congregation only appear as the service begins. We rely heavily on the vicar to sing up when it is an unfamiliar hymn.

What about the 'Can't sing, won't sing' brigade? Here again subtle methods are required. Many of our congregation and others will be persuaded to join in a community drama of some sort. Nearly a thousand took part in 'The Greenwich Passion Play 2000' in Greenwich Park, and people who would not normally attend a choir practice came to rehearsals, which included singing.

## Personal development and support

Having coped with the parish musical requirements, just how does the parish musician fit in time for their own development? Despite common belief to the contrary, private practice time is necessary for all musicians regardless of their capabilities, and creating time for this requires skill, discipline and efficiency (including delegation where possible). Support and encouragement are essential: comments from the congregation which indicate that they really did listen to the voluntary you spent weeks practising can be a real incentive to a musician. Meeting with other musicians to share the good and the bad is really helpful and can be a wonderful opportunity to pool resources and gain fresh enthusiasm. Parishes need to be aware that various lessons, lectures and courses are available if only the time and finances can be secured, and musicians often need help and encouragement to access them. Identifying people for training as musicians in a parish should be planned in the same way as we look for Readers, Southwark Pastoral Auxiliaries or Ordained Local Ministers. Don't wait until the organist has left for university or is in training for the ministry. At St George's youngsters who are learning to play instruments are encouraged to take part in a service by playing during communion, providing a voluntary, or joining with the orchestra. This is challenging for me as I have to incorporate them into the rota, make time to rehearse them, ensure that the shy ones are asked if they don't volunteer, and make sure that everyone has equal opportunities. As we have a growing number of musicians I am very grateful to several adults who have taken on some of the responsibilities when they saw that I was struggling, and we meet regularly to plan with our vicar.

## Christian musician

I may be the parish musician but I am also a Christian and the parish needs to be aware of this. I find it very difficult to join in all aspects of worship while 'working', so I need to find times for my own spirituality. In some parishes assistants are engaged to allow the regular musician personal worship time, and services can be planned without the need for the regular musician. A nearby colleague told me that in their parish worship planning meetings begin with an act of worship for the musicians. Occasionally I escape to services where I'm not being the musician. This is good for my own spirituality, and I might also find fresh inspiration for my ministry of music.

How happy are the people who worship you with songs. (Psalm 89.15)

There are many criticisms about music in worship, and particularly about church music not appealing to today's people. It is a challenge not only for the parish musician, the minister and the worship leader, but for all Christians, to keep the people who worship 'happy'.

## Further reading

Dunstan, Alan, *The Use of Hymns*, Kevin Mayhew, Suffolk, 1990.
Mackenzie, Ian, *Tunes of Glory – what music is good enough for God?* Handsel Press, Scotland, 1993.
Archbishops' Commission on Church Music, *In Tune with Heaven*, Church House Publishing, London, 1992.

## 10.  Children Among Us
### The Children's Church Teacher

ALISON SEAMAN

At that time the disciples came to Jesus and asked, 'Who is the greatest in the kingdom of heaven?' He called a child, whom he put among them, and said, 'Truly I tell you, unless you change and become like children, you will never enter the kingdom of heaven. Whoever becomes humble like this child is the greatest in the kingdom of heaven. Whoever welcomes one such child in my name welcomes me.' (Matthew 18.3–5)

### Why do children always ask difficult questions?

We were setting the scene for a children's Advent Workshop. About 30 children, aged between about 4 and 11, sat in a circle around me. I told the story of the Christmas season: there was a felt underlay that was ceremoniously unfolded and the wooden figures of Mary and Joseph, the shepherds and the Magi were carefully set out. Finally, a little wooden figure of the Christchild was placed in the manger. The whole presentation illustrated the journey to Bethlehem. The children watched as the story unfolded in front of them. I looked up at them; this was a story they knew well but they were engaged and interested. I asked, 'I wonder what part of this story you think is most important?'

Animals are always a popular feature of this type of discussion. The wise man's camel was a particular favourite.

Some thought the shepherd's sheep, and some thought Mary's donkey was the star of the show. To be fair, Jesus did get a mention, and one of the children said he thought the journey to Bethlehem was the most important part of the story. I began to relax; the children knew the Christmas story and were beginning to grapple with its meaning. Then it came – out of the blue. A silent, rather serious child looked directly at me and said, 'Yes, but is it all really true?' There was a long silence. I tried to look calm and thoughtful but those who know me well recognized that under the surface I was thinking, 'What on earth do I say now?' I took a deep breath and replied, 'I sometimes think about that too. I wonder if there are things around us here in Church that will help us all think more about your question.' And they were away. Challenging each other, making suggestions, hypothesizing, encouraging; going deeper and deeper into the mystery of incarnation . . . 4-to-11-year-olds doing theology. I was now the one to sit back and watch in awe and wonder. In this situation, as on many other previous occasions, I found myself asking: Who is the teacher and who is the learner?

There seems to be a presumption that we have to fill children, like empty vessels, until they are brimming to the surface with information *about* religion; we have to *teach* them to be more like *us*. If, however, we are to take Jesus' words about the Kingdom of God to heart (Matthew 18.3–5), are we not being challenged to turn the tables on this common perception? Should we not be asking ourselves: How can *we* become more like *them*? What can *we* learn by listening to *them*?

### The rollercoaster of children's work

Working with children in church is always a journey of discovery. Challenging and demanding, no two weeks ever being the same, it can be a rollercoaster of joys and frustrations, highs and lows, moments of stillness and noisy activity, as children come and go week by week. So how are children being encouraged to develop their role in the Church family?

What are the practicalities of being a children's church teacher? Who are the people who participate in children's work?[1]

This chapter outlines some of the experiences of a small sample of parishes in south-east London where children's ministry operates. No two churches are the same: in church tradition, in the size and make-up of congregation, or in financial circumstances. The stories they offer are particular to their setting. All have experienced successes and failures, weeks when everything seems to work like clockwork and weeks when even the most carefully prepared session seems to descend into chaos. The examples of practice are not offered as the right or only way to work, rather as ways or approaches that have worked best in our situations.

## Being with children

Many of the people I meet who are involved with children's church work already had some relationship with children, maybe as parents or grandparents, but many didn't have. I have always been involved with children in my professional life as a teacher and education adviser. A decision to work freelance gave me the flexibility to become more involved with children's work at my own church, Holy Trinity in Eltham. In my job I had spent time exploring the whole area of children's religious and spiritual development but, ironically, I found I had little direct contact with them: it was a case of knowing the theory but not having much practice. I now had the opportunity to work on a more regular basis with children and my motivation was very much to learn from them about how best to serve their needs at Holy Trinity.

## Building the ethos: church or school?

Adults attend church for a myriad of reasons: the time and space to be still, to pray and give thanks, and to learn and grow in faith, come high on many people's lists of attractions to church. There is also the importance of meeting with friends and having the support of a caring community. So what brings children to church? For many, of course, they come to church because they are brought, but for children, too, being with their friends and learning and worshipping together all have their appeal.

Bearing all this in mind, in one of our regular reviews of children's work at Holy Trinity we gave some thought to the range of experiences the children were being offered in our community. We could identify plenty of opportunities for children to meet together, build friendships and have fun, and these were seen to be the essential groundwork for maintaining a thriving children's church. The provision for the children's Christian education came through a structured learning programme that formed the basis of each Sunday morning session. On arrival at church children were welcomed into the adjacent church hall, listened to Bible stories, participated in creative activities, and then joined the rest of the congregation for communion.

Identifying the children's opportunities for worship was, however, less easy. They said prayers and sang songs, but were they engaging in the rich multi-sensory experiences of worship that were on offer for everyone else in our community? On reflection, it seemed that the children's experience of church mainly focused on learning; literally a Sunday *school* where the children could be with friends and learn *about* Christianity. Were we nurturing them sufficiently in the language and experience of Christian worship?

## Creating sacred space: ritual and liturgy

We decided that providing a separate worship space for the children on most Sundays was, for our church, still the best way forward; but we wanted to ensure that their worship should feel part of a whole rather than an add-on. We embarked on some practical and organizational changes in order to make this shift. We wanted to maintain a happy, welcoming community where learning together was an essential part of our culture, but we now wanted to explore ways of rooting this in the worship traditions of our church.

The first major change was to bring children into church for the beginning of the service, rather than going straight into Sunday Club. As the choir and clergy enter, the children now join the end of the procession and follow it to the altar. Here they are presented with a cross, a Bible and a banner (made by the children), which then form the head of the children's procession into their meeting areas. This relatively simple ritual has ensured not only that children are visible to all present, but also that they are actively participating in the ritual of worship from the beginning of the service.

Processing into their meeting rooms they find the space prepared with a worship area and an activity area. (There are currently three groups of children that meet each week in three different locations.) As the children enter each of the rooms, they have ahead of them a small table to act as a focus for their worship space. This is covered with a cloth in the appropriate liturgical colour and a candle. The children leading the procession place the Bible and cross on the table, everyone settles around the table, and the session begins.

A simple liturgy has been devised. The children begin by making the sign of the cross, and a standard greeting is used. One of a range of 'sorry songs' is sung and at appropriate times of year this is followed by a simple musical setting of the Gloria. The children then engage with the Bible story, usually the Gospel reading for the day, in a variety of ways including storytelling, discussion, drama, music, and art and craft activities. There is then movement around the room as the children work on different activities.

The oldest group of children (aged 8+) return into church for the Peace. The younger children have a little more time for activities before everyone gathers again in the worship area for a short prayer before processing back into church (with the Bible, cross and banner leading the way). Here the children receive a blessing or communion and remain in church for the final part of the service.

There have been other practical developments that have evolved over time. The support materials used by the teachers were changed to a publication that follows the lectionary readings.[2] Teachers were formed into teams and the decision was made to work in blocks of Sundays (approximately a month at a time) to give greater continuity of practice and to help the planning and organization. It was also decided to offer worship for children throughout the year. This was another way of trying to redirect the ethos of children's church away from the 'school' model: worship was something that happened all year round, not just in the school terms. All of these developments were aimed at encouraging children to feel at ease and be familiar with the worship traditions of their church. When they participate in church services they are now familiar with the style and pattern of worship and the ritual becomes second nature.

## Children at the heart of the Church

St George's Church in Westcombe Park is, like Holy Trinity, a community where children's work now plays a vital role in the life of the church. But this was not always the case. When Julie Mason's children were very young there was little on offer for them and so she faced the decision of either moving on or organizing something for them herself. She decided on the latter and with a group of parents organized activities for their children during the Sunday morning service. Over the years this has grown into a children's church and there are now enough children for three different age groups, each meeting in separate rooms, during the first part of the Sunday morning service. The groups have a leader and a helper, working on a rota system, so that the responsibility of working with children is shared. The leaders use the *Living Stones*[3] series to help plan activities for each session. The resources provide ideas and an outline for each Sunday but as the leaders increase in confidence they often start to devise their own ideas. A pattern has emerged over time: a welcome activity to gather the children together (this offers some flexibility as not all the children arrive punctually); reading/telling the Bible story of the day (usually the Gospel reading); a worksheet-based activity; and ending with a short prayer. Experience has shown that the younger children's groups tend to focus on becoming familiar with Bible stories; with older children, the focus tends to shift to more discussion work.

For some time now, children have rejoined the service in church at the Peace. They follow the service using children's communion books[4] and older children will often help the younger ones to follow the proceedings.

## Developing worship for all

Children's work seems to require a fine balance between recognizing the needs of children to have time together and be themselves in their own space while also providing opportunities for them to play their role as part of a larger community. This became the crux of the discussions at St Thomas's, Charlton when the congregation came to review the pattern of worship that was being offered to both adults and children in the church. St Thomas's has a small congregation and the Parochial Church Council (PCC) discussed whether to offer 'all age' style worship each week or whether to develop the children's church model and offer separate worship for children and young people for part of the service each week.

They soon realized that no one had discussed the issue with the children themselves in order to discover *their* views. A consultation process was set up by Liz Newman who, as a relatively new member of the congregation, felt she could take a relatively neutral stance on the subject. The outcome of the consultation was that the children wanted to have a separate space and time together: something special for them. But there was also a sense in which they did not want to miss out on the church service. Children in this congregation felt that they belonged and they were keen to preserve that. In the children's work that is developing at St Thomas's the child's voice is valued and heard.

St George's and Holy Trinity both have a tradition of maintaining a 'both/and' model: running a children's church and holding regular 'all age'-style services. St George's holds all age services on the first Sunday of every month, as well as on major festivals. Julie Mason and other children's church teachers organize these services, working closely with the vicar and parish musician. The children participate fully by reading, saying prayers, and offering music. Services like this require a great deal of preparation but are seen as being an essential way in which children feel part of the process of building community at St George's.

At Holy Trinity there had been a pattern of holding all age-style services at major festival times and gradually, with the support and interest of clergy and lay readers and church musicians, these have increased in number and now take place approximately once a month. Children take an active part in these services, working alongside adults to sing in the choir, read lessons and lead intercessions, and often to participate in the 'sermon slot'. The aim of these services was to include all of our children, but over time, and through consultation with both children and adults, it became clear that the very youngest children were still finding it difficult to engage with the all age service. So we decided to return to offering separate worship sessions for the youngest children during all age services (except for Easter Day and Christmas Day). This was not an easy decision, and as ever in such situations meant having to balance the interests of everyone involved. Creating meaningful and worshipful experiences for people of all ages will always be a tall order, but trying to do so has required us to reflect upon the fact that children, like adults, often need their own time and space within the communal activities that create Sunday morning worship.

## Dealing with the practicalities

I once joked to a member of our congregation that co-ordinating children's work was more about making sure the register is taken and tidying up the art materials cupboard than being with children. Although an exaggeration of reality, this points to the fact that there are important practical issues to be addressed when working with children and the range of tasks that stem from this are best shared among a group of people. An example of this, at Holy Trinity, is our response to The Children Act. We have a child protection representative and she prepared a policy for the protection of children and vulnerable adults. She has ensured, among other things, that all of our volunteers who are in contact with children are checked by the Criminal Records Bureau, registers are kept whenever the children meet, and volunteers receive training in good practice in working with children. For volunteers who are new to children's work this can all seem rather demanding at first, but our experience has been that keeping people well-informed, and offering training, reassures them, particularly when they realize that the process offers protection not only to those children to whom we minister but also to those who freely offer their time and talents to further that ministry.

## Working with people's gifts

Co-ordinating children's work at Holy Trinity is made straightforward by having in place a large group of committed people willing to work with children on Sunday mornings. One of the hardest lessons to be learned by anyone working with children is that one person neither can nor should do everything, and that working in a team is essential for people working in children's ministry. This takes time to evolve. At Holy Trinity, having the clergy and staff team on board was essential to the work. It means that the process is part of the work of the whole church. To have the parish priest, curate and

Readers working with the children and supporting teachers on a regular basis gives a clear message that children's work is important.

At St Thomas's, too, clergy and Readers are being encouraged to get involved with children's work. The retirement of a long-standing children's church teacher required the church to review the worship provision offered to children and young people. Time is being given to broaden interest in children's ministry and to create a greater sense of ownership by the whole community. Significantly, a budget has been agreed by the PCC and an assessment made of the human resources required to ensure that the work can go ahead. Information has been prepared for the congregation informing them of developments and encouraging them to sponsor the purchase of some new materials.

Discovering people's gifts forms an essential part of co-ordinating the work of children's church teachers. This includes the vital recognition that for some people their gift is *not* working with children – and this goes for lay people *and* clergy.

It is important to discover the natural leaders and those who prefer to take supporting roles; the storytellers, the art-ists, the organizers, the listeners. Volunteers usually need encouragement and reassurance. Some will have a church-going background with a strong faith and be very committed to Christian nurture of children. Some may be relatively new to church or might be rediscovering a church background and so are embarking on a journey of faith and discovery along-side their children. Many children's church teachers have a sense of wanting to 'do their bit' and wanting to ensure the best possible experience for the children in the church.

Some of the volunteers at Holy Trinity have experience of working with children in a professional capacity but the majority would consider themselves to be laypeople in this regard. While it is tempting to encourage education profes-sionals into children's work this may not be the best thing for them but they will often be very useful supporters and might

willingly offer help and advice. At St Thomas's, experience
has shown that people need to be asked and encouraged to
help with children's work. Volunteers can be concerned that
they will not 'know enough' and they might need reassurance
that they do not need to be experts. Using good resources
and offering background material for preparation can help
teachers to further their own faith development. A particularly important step is when a teacher recognizes that they do
not need to know the answer to every question.


## Seeing things differently

At St George's, Julie Mason became involved with children's
work because no one else was doing any work with children
when she had young children of her own. Having built up a
thriving children's church, she feels it has played a significant
part in her own faith journey. She has learned from children
the importance of simplicity and is often inspired by what
they say. She recognizes that the work she does is making an
important contribution to the life of her church, indeed, to the
future of the Church.

Julie and I are both closely involved with preparing children
for first communion. In our churches this is offered to children
when they are seven. Working alongside them as they approach
this important milestone in their faith journey is one of the
great privileges of being a children's church teacher. We find
ourselves revisiting ideas that we have not thought about for
some time: it is a chance to see things differently or in a new
light. We often find ourselves saying 'I'd never thought about
that before'. We also find that we are sometimes asking the
children to challenge their experience in other aspects of their
lives. In a recent first communion group one of the children
asked, with some anxiety in her voice, if there would be a test
at the end? To be told 'No' was quite a shock: she is growing
up in a world where everyone has targets to reach, hurdles to
jump. Already in her life God's love, freely given, seems too
good to be true.

So why are we children's church teachers? Because we like to learn, and because we're in the business of building communities where children can thrive. We want to create safe spaces where they can think big, make connections, be open to the unexpected and, most important, feel free to ask those difficult questions. By listening to children we are blessed by seeing with new eyes the presence of God in our own lives, and we find our spiritual journeys deepened and nourished.

## Further reading

Bunge, M. J. (ed.), *The Child in Christian Thought*, Eerdmans, Grand Rapids/Cambridge, 2001.

Berryman, J. W., *How to Lead Godly Play Lessons*, *The Complete Guide to Godly Play Series*, Volume 1, Living the Good News, Denver, Colorado, 2002.

Williams, R. D., *Lost Icons: Reflections on Cultural Bereavement*, Chapter 1, 'Children and choice', T. & T. Clark, London, 2000.

## Notes

1 Churches use a variety of terms for those who lead and support children's activities in church. In this chapter 'children's church teacher' is used. The term 'children's work' principally refers to Sunday morning worship, while recognizing that children's church teachers are often involved in other activities for children, for example at festival times, in the school holidays and, in some cases, in weekday after school clubs.

2 *Seasons of the Spirit* is a Christian education curriculum published by Wood Lake Books, Kelowma, BC, Canada. It is distributed in the UK by Cornerstone Bookshops in Edinburgh (phone 0131 229 3776) or Glasgow (phone 0141 353 3776) or online *www.cornerstonebooks. org.uk*.

3 Sayers, S., *Living Stones*, Kevin Mayhew 1998, a series of resources for children's work following the Revised Common Lectionary.

4 Murrie, D., *My Communion Book*, Church House Publishing, London, 2002.

# 11. Keeping Us Young
## The Youth Leader

### BRIDGET SHEPHERD

Remember your creator in the days of your youth.
(Ecclesiastes 12.1a)

## From the sublime to the ridiculous

Last night I spent half an hour sweeping up squashed Wotsits and wiping shaving foam off the furniture, while trying to think how I'd explain *another* broken light to the church hall caretaker. That was the aftermath of Fishcake (don't ask about the name), one of the church youth groups. About five minutes before the end of Fishcake, I'd decided that I hated youth work, hated young people, and wanted to develop a ministry with the over 65s! That was until Ian – one of the young people – saved the day. We'd spent the evening thinking about the commandment 'You shall not covet'. The young people had been uninterested, unresponsive and uncontrollable. Then Ian said something really profound and really helpful, and everyone really listened. I could have kissed him (if it hadn't been for our child protection policy). Suddenly it all felt worthwhile again.

Later that evening a young person, whose father had recently died, popped into church. We spent a while sitting together in silence, then talking, and finally we prayed together. It was a precious moment – then she offered me a chocolate Penguin! Working with young people often takes you from the sublime to the ridiculous, and back again, in a short space of time.

Whatever your situation, youth work has to be done. Whether you've got a group of kids throwing stones at the window, a group of parents demanding activities for their offspring, or a bunch of young people in the back pew, youth work is necessary. But what do we mean when we talk about youth work?

## What is youth work?

Youth work can take a variety of forms. Activities may be primarily for 'churched' young people, or for 'unchurched' young people. They may be focused on discipleship, or focused on evangelism. They may be more formal, or less formal. They may be based in your church premises, or detached. Let me give you a few examples of the sort of youth work you might come across in the parish.

Sue and Jo run the youth group at their church. Sue is the mum of three of the girls in the group. She started running the group because she felt that the teenagers in church needed it, and about a dozen young people come along now. They meet together twice a month on Sunday evenings at Sue's home. The programme is usually based on that day's Gospel reading, although from time to time they like to vary things: before Lent they made pancakes, in Advent they sold home-made crafts for charity, and next year they're planning a 'sleep out' to raise money for a youth homelessness organization. Sue is delighted as two of the group have now become youth leaders, and she thinks they might soon have to find a hall to meet in.

All Saints is a small, poorly resourced church in an Urban Priority Area. Every Friday they run Rock Solid, a group for 12-year-olds and upwards. Most of the young people who come live on the local estate, and apart from Rock Solid they have nothing to do with the church. Each week the youth leaders choose a theme for the evening, then the young people play games, undertake activities and hold discussions based on it. Last year they even took some of the Rock Solid kids to a summer camp. All Saints would love to do more work with local young people, but they can't because they don't have the youth leaders or the money to do it.

Charlie is the new minister at the Holy Spirit Church. Recently a large group of young people from the estate where the church is based forced their way in during one of the services. They were abusive and aggressive and 'helped themselves' to the fellowship tea that the small congregation was sharing. Charlie and his wife Sarah aren't thinking about starting a 'youth group', at this stage they just want to build a positive link with the young people. Then they'll see where things go from there.

St Bartholomew's has employed several youth workers over the past ten years. They have around 70 young people who come to the youth groups. They tend to focus on Christian young people, and their groups revolve around exploring the Bible, praying and worshipping together, and 'having a laugh'. The youth leaders take the young people away several times a year, run all sorts of social events for them, and encourage them to get involved in outreach, mission and service, wherever and whenever they can.

St Nicholas's is a small church with a handful of youngsters, but on a church parade Sunday there could be as many as 60 children and young people there. The vicar at St Nick's is really pleased to have several uniformed organizations linked to the church; he's also keen that the church should develop its own evangelistic youth work. There is a lot of potential for developing the work with young people in the parish – but the starting point is working out a strategy for what they'd like to do.

Church-based youth work can take many different forms, but what is it that makes it distinctive from secular youth work? Church youth work is Christ-centred, and is about bringing young people to faith in Jesus Christ. It may have other aims and objectives along the way – inclusion, education, empowerment, and so on – but it is ultimately focused on enabling young people to discover and encounter Christ for themselves. While other aims are valid and valuable, it is Christ – not youth leaders or youth programmes – who has the power to transform young people's lives. As transformation takes place, those other aims may well be realized 'in Christ'.

All the youth leaders in the examples above are working towards that same end – albeit in different ways and with different types of young people. As far as I'm concerned, the Church is central to the task of bringing young people to Christ, and is the best place for faith to be nurtured and extended. But does that mean that we need specific youth work?

## Why do youth work?

I first got involved in youth work as a young person, running the Christian Union at my school and doing outreach work to other young people in a nearby town. I wanted to do youth work for several reasons: because I'd been inspired by youth leaders in the past, because it was an area of Christian service where I could 'have a go', and most of all because I sensed that God was calling me into ministry with young people. When I left school at 18 I spent my gap year with a Christian organization doing youth work and evangelism, and a year out became a life out! Since then my ideas and methods have evolved, but my passion for young people and youth work remains just as strong.

When I asked a number of clergy and youth leaders why they run youth work in their churches, I got a variety of responses. But more than anything else, they all said the same thing, 'It has to be done'. But *why* does it have to be done?

## The mission of the Church

Youth work has to be done because it's part of the mission of the Church. The Church's mission is to proclaim by word and deed the creative and redemptive activity of God. This mission is rooted in the incarnation, initiated by the Spirit and conducted in a specific context and culture. Youth work is therefore mission in the context of youth culture: it is aimed specifically at adolescents, addresses the issues that concern them, and does that in a way which is authentic and relevant to them. The Church needs to be faithful in passing on the unchanging elements of Christian belief and lifestyle, while at the same time empowering young people to work out the application of those elements for their own context.

In my experience, it is the youth leader's role to 'translate' between the cultural context of young people in the church community and the cultural context of the adults. Young people may not understand or connect with some of the ways in which adults articulate and demonstrate their faith, so the youth leader needs to translate what they're doing, and to work in partnership with them to find expressions of faith that they can understand and connect with.

I help to run a youth group called Legacy. They love comedy, have a great sense of humour, and manage to see the funny side of everything. When we come to discuss 'God and stuff' they apply the same sense of humour to the topic in hand – which makes for a somewhat irreverent brand of humour. If some of the people in church heard the jokes they make then they'd probably be quite offended; but the jokes aren't intended to be offensive. It's just that that's how young people bring a subject to life and apply it to their lives.

Youth work is frequently innovative, and youth leaders are helping to develop new forms of discipleship, worship and church structure that will one day become the mainstream. In the meantime, I hope that their missionary efforts will enable young people and adults to learn and benefit from one another, and to grow together as members of the body of Christ.

## Entertainment and engagement

The second reason for doing youth work is because it works. You don't *have* to have a youth leader or a youth group for young people to be welcomed and included in the worshipping life of the Church; but young people are more likely to remain in the Church and make the transition from adolescent faith to adult faith if there is special provision for them.

Churches often feel obliged to provide activities for young people as an antidote to boredom; either boredom induced by the services, or by the lack of amenities in the local area. So is the role of the youth leader essentially that of an entertainer, or is it something more than that? I think that youth work is effective because it seeks to *engage* young people, not *entertain* them. The youth leader isn't a free babysitter for Friday nights or Sunday mornings: their role is to find age-appropriate ways to get young people thinking, discussing and learning about the Christian story. As part of that learning process they may use entertainment to get them and keep them interested, but it's not an end in itself.

Mark's dad gets really annoyed with the youth leader at St Bart's. When Mark's dad was young they never played games and messed around but *he* still came to church. He would prefer it if the youth leader just taught the young people about the Bible, and cut out all the silliness. But Mark really enjoys it, and he seems to be learning a lot too. This term the youth leader has been helping them to think about mission, and next term they'll be studying Revelation. Mark's dad may not approve, but Mark and his mates certainly do.

Many people come to faith in their teenage years. Whether that reflects the specific efforts of youth leaders, or some characteristic of adolescence, I don't know, but it is worth investing time, energy and resources into youth work because young people *do* respond favourably. And now more than ever we need to be capitalizing on their postmodern fascination with all things 'spiritual'.

## Maintenance and development

It doesn't take a genius to work out that if the numbers of young people coming to church continue to diminish then it won't be long before our churches are empty! Youth ministry is vital if we still want to see Church in the future. This presents us with two challenges: the need to *maintain* the number of young people attending church groups, and the need to *develop* the work our churches do in order to increase the numbers of young people who are part of them.

When Tim joined St Nicholas's, the youth work was at a low ebb. He decided that he needed to do something straight away, so he started a youth group to try and keep hold of the seven young people who were still involved with the church. Tim describes the group as being 'very basic' and involving 'a lot of mucking about'. He really wants to grow the group, but he doesn't know where to start. Tim is quite self-deprecating about the youth work at St Nick's; but as far as I'm concerned he has a great deal to celebrate – because the church has successfully held on to the seven.

Leah has been working for St Michael's for six months as their full-time Youth and Children's Worker. When she started the job she was given a long list of young people who had been part of the church at one time or another but no longer came to the groups. She sent out dozens of invitations and information leaflets, and made countless phone calls to parents and their children, but the young people still wouldn't come to the youth group. A few weeks ago she organized a youth-led service followed by an ice-skating trip – and 17 of them came. The week after the ice-skating trip the youth group was back to the usual six girls, and Leah was back to the drawing board. Leah has a lot to think through, but is very excited about the possibilities of increasing her contact with this group and expanding and adapting the programme of youth activities.

Church youth work *can* be and *is* successful at maintaining and developing contact with young people – however big or small, basic or sophisticated, 'professional' or 'amateur' that work happens to be. The key is prayerfully persisting until you find what works in your particular setting, as Tim and Leah are both discovering.

In a lot of cases youth work is a long-term investment, and the fruit may not be seen for many years, if at all. A significant number of young people will end up leaving the Church, but that doesn't mean that they won't be back, or that God is no longer part of their lives. Only this week, the church I attend has welcomed two new members – both of whom attended churches as teenagers then subsequently left. While it's important to avoid complacency about the numbers of young people in our churches, we need to remember that youth work isn't about 'bums on pews'. Whether young people profess faith and remain regular churchgoers, or not, we shouldn't underestimate the legacy of youth work.

## How do you do youth work?

I recently met a man who's been working with young people since the 1950s and is still going strong. He doesn't look like you might imagine a youth worker to look: he has long white hair and a long white beard (rather like an ageing Klingon) and he still dresses like a Teddy Boy. While his wardrobe is past its best, his ideas are bang up to date.

Youth work can be done in lots of different ways by lots of different people. Each church needs to work out what's right for its own particular setting, and how it can make the most of the people and resources available to it. If you're thinking about getting some youth work going but don't know where to start, you could contact your diocesan youth officer. They will be able to help you with recruitment, training, child protection, supervision, and so on, or they might simply recommend some materials that might be of use to you. But whoever you are, whatever you end up doing, the following general principles apply across all settings.

### There's no such thing as a second-hand faith

Youth work isn't just about passing on *your* understanding of God, it's about enabling young people to experience and encounter God for themselves. In my mind that means three things: that we value and validate people's questions; that we support them as they work out what being a Christian is about; and that we create or find settings that help them to sense God's presence. Let me give you three examples.

1. One Sunday morning I was leading a session with a group of 10- to 12-year-olds on Sodom and Gomorrah. The story got them thinking and they began to ask lots of questions . . . why is there suffering in the world? Will everyone go to heaven? Where did the world come from? And so on. Rather than trying to keep them on track with the teaching material we'd prepared, we abandoned our plans and spent time discussing *their* questions.

2. One Sunday evening Legacy, an older youth group, were doing a session on sex. At the end of the evening one of the girls wanted to talk further, so she arranged to meet up with a leader mid-week to chat things through. The leader didn't tell her what to do or not do; she just listened and tried to help the girl to find God's perspective.

3. Many of the young people I've worked with find it easiest to 'feel' that God is real when they attend big Christian events. Every year we make sure we do something that offers them the opportunity to go to a big event – even if the leaders aren't madly keen on going. But we also stress that God is near to them in the ordinary things we do, week in, week out.

Our job as youth leaders is essentially to watch what God is doing in the lives of young people, and then to join in. Doing youth work is vitally important, but the success of that work depends on the Holy Spirit. In that respect faith is caught, not taught; so I do all that I can to make our church and the various youth groups we run an 'infectious environment'.

## The importance of getting them involved

If you want to give young people a reason to be in church, then give them a job! It doesn't matter what the job is – doing the collection, helping run junior church, being involved with the music, or doing the sermon (it has been known). Giving people an appropriate job helps them to fit in and belong, and it gives them a stake in what is going on. The Church is, after all, the body of Christ, and we need all the parts we can get. Young people may well be young, but they still have a great deal to offer.

The parish of St James is in a largely middle-class area, with a sister church on a nearby council estate. The young people from Quest and Flame, the youth groups at St James's, heard about a children's club being run on the estate. Several of them asked if they could get involved as helpers, and they have been going along ever since. The young people have helped to strengthen the links between the two churches and to encourage the bigger church to support the work of the smaller. Best of all, they've learned lots from the sister church while they've been serving it.

Even if we're unable or unsure about giving young people roles and responsibilities, we need to make sure that our churches are places that encourage activity, not passivity, as 'having a go' can be one of the best ways to learn about being a Christian. And this doesn't just apply to the young people . . .

Helen went to church as a child, but stopped going when she got older. She decided to go back to church in her early twenties as she wanted a church wedding. When the youth worker did an appeal for new volunteers, Helen responded. She joined the team of youth leaders at the church, and got involved in planning and leading meetings. Having a go at youth work helped Helen to rediscover her own faith; and it was pretty inspiring for the young people to witness the whole process too.

## The centrality of relationships

Experience has shown me that at the heart of all good youth work are good relationships between youth leaders and young people. If we want to engage with teenagers then we need to get to know them as *people*. If we want to talk about faith in a meaningful way with young people, then we need to form a connection with them. We might connect over football, or fashion, or film, or even farming. That connection opens up a genuine dialogue between young people and us, and it's in the context of that genuine dialogue that we can begin to talk with them about life and faith. Knowing something about young people's backgrounds and interests also helps us to care for them better – for example, it's no good teaching about 'the family of God' if we don't know what family means to them.

Sarah is a new volunteer youth leader at the church I attend. In my capacity as youth worker I've asked her to start a small Bible study group for some older girls. She's tried on several occasions to get this group of busy young women together, but for one reason or another they've been unable to make it. In the end Sarah gave up trying and decided to go shopping with them instead. By the time they'd 'done' Oxford Street all the girls had got to know Sarah and were keen to get going with the group.

Relationships with young people aren't just one-way: they are two-way. As well as getting to know young people, youth leaders need to allow young people to get to know them – within certain boundaries of course. When young people get to know their youth leaders their understanding of faith moves from theory to practice as they see how being a Christian works in reality. The way of life that the youth leader models may be far more powerful at communicating the gospel than any meeting that they ever run.

## Conclusion

Youth work is immensely valuable: for the young people, for their families, for the wider church family, for the community as a whole, and for the youth leaders themselves. As a young person I valued youth work because it was fun, I made friends through it, and it introduced me to God. As an adult I value youth work because it helps to keep the Church feeling fresh and full of promise.

I never wanted to be a church youth worker. In fact I thought it would be the worst job imaginable (I think I even used the words: 'A mug's game'). It turns out that I love it, and that I think it's the *best* job imaginable. Young people are simultaneously creative *and* unimaginative, active *and* apathetic, profound *and* superficial, concerned for the needs of others *and* utterly self-obsessed. I find them intensely frustrating to work with, and yet completely compelling.

I can't imagine anything better than hearing a young person profess faith in Christ for the first time, and then tell you about their new trainers.

### *Further reading*

Hickford, Andy, *Essential Youth: Why the Church Needs Young People*, Spring Harvest & Authentic Lifestyle, Carlisle, 2003.

Brierley, Danny, *What Every Volunteer Youth Worker Should Know*, Spring Harvest & Authentic Lifestyle, Carlisle, 2003

Fields, Doug, *Purpose-Driven Youth Ministry: 9 Essential Foundations for Healthy Growth*, Zondervan, Grand Rapids, 1998.

See also: www.youthwork.co.uk

# 12. Serving in the Economy
## The Workplace Chaplain

### MALCOLM TORRY

With what can we compare the kingdom of God, or what parable will we use for it? It is like a mustard seed, which, when sown upon the ground, is the smallest of all the seeds on earth; yet when it is sown it grows up and becomes the greatest of all shrubs, and puts forth large branches, so that the birds of the air can make nests in its shade. (Mark 4.30–32)

About once a month I walk down Westcombe Hill, across Woolwich Road, along Tunnel Avenue, and into Tate & Lyle: the food refinery on the Greenwich Peninsula. If I pass someone on the way in, they might say hello or if they're a visitor themselves they might wonder why there's someone in a dog collar on the site and they won't know whether to say hello or not.

I sign the book, show my identity pass, go to the locker-room, change into thick socks and steel-capped boots, put on an orange jacket, put safety-goggles and ear-protectors in my pocket, take my helmet in my hand, and head for the canteen.

When I started visiting the refinery nine years ago the canteen would have been fairly full at about ten in the morning, and outside contractors had a different set of times so they didn't get in the way of Tate & Lyle's own people. Several waves of redundancies, both voluntary and otherwise, have made the separate times unnecessary and the notice has disappeared. Now I can find myself sitting with Tate & Lyle staff on one side and contractors on the other.

We talk about the company, the weather, politics, God, their families – whatever comes up. And then a mobile phone will ring and a fitter will go to fix a valve, a process worker will go back to their computer screen, a lab technician will go to continue quality tests – and I'll set about visiting the site: the wheat plant, where the wheat comes in from the company's mill in East Anglia and is processed and passed to other parts of the plant; the control rooms of the parts of the refinery, which make different sugar products; the starch centrifuges (ear-protectors needed); the power plant (the refinery has its own gas-fired power station); the fitters' shop, the electricians, the stores, the offices – though the offices don't take as long as they used to since most of the financial functions were moved to the group's headquarters in Belgium and other functions to the Tate & Lyle sugar refinery across the river.

If I go into a control room and there's no one there or they're all clearly occupied then I'll leave and return later, but often people have five minutes for a chat. And if it's tea-break time in the fitters' rest-room then they'll talk for longer, feet up, discussing what's in the papers that morning, or some recent change in the plant's management culture, or the state of the trades unions, or the traffic jams on the Blackwall Tunnel approach road. Someone might tell me about someone else's bereavement and I'll make time to talk to the person bereaved, or they might seek me out. Or maybe an argument in a tea-room or a control room will get heated (some subjects are almost bound to produce this effect), and finding the right time and the right line to end on is crucial.

The Chamber of Commerce has its office on the site, and if there's time then I'll drop in. And beyond that is the transport depot, where sometimes the drivers are waiting for their loads to be ready. And beyond that again is the distillery, which makes alcohol out of the products left over from the production of starch, glucose and other sweeteners. Occasionally I'll help with the crossword: a source of some interesting conversations.

The rule is always the same: I never repeat to anyone else what someone tells me – which is why they tell me in the first place. Which isn't to say that what I hear on one month's visit might not provide some of the content of my questions on the next, whether those questions are about rotas, safety, the state of the sugar market, the euro, trades unions, death, despair, or celebration.

I always have lunch in the canteen and will try to sit with someone I don't know – which often means a contractor: there are more of these now that the company has shed quite a lot of its own fitters and electricians. And again the conversations will be diverse: children's schools, holidays, a colleague's illness, Christmas . . . As people leave the table there will sometimes be one person left, and the conversation might touch on more sensitive issues.

Sometimes I'm there for three hours, sometimes for five or more, and throughout it is pastoral care, in the sense that a representative of the Church is attempting to relate the gospel to the situation in which we find ourselves. This is not an exercise in evangelism, and on some visits the name of God will not be mentioned and the only discussion of the Church will be me trying not to defend the indefensible behaviour of Christians past and present. But sometimes I'm asked clear questions about the Christian faith; often the deepest theological conversations will emerge from discussion of last weekend's visit to the grandchildren; occasionally I'll be asked to answer for a faith other than my own; and sometimes I'm challenged on why I'm there in the first place: I'm there as a guest, to listen, to speak from within the faith tradition of which I am a servant (and to respect others' faith positions), and to contribute to mutual understanding between the Church and industry, commerce and other institutions in the economy.

Because I am a guest I exercise the obvious courtesies: I don't discuss the company's current issues outside the plant, except in the most general terms (as in this chapter); I don't pass on sensitive information I overhear; and if I have a genuine concern about some issue (whether it be safety, the treatment of a particular individual, a company policy, or whatever) then I never break confidences – though I might raise a general question with the manager concerned on the basis of my own observations, not on the basis of what someone might have said to me.

When I've been round the site I put my boots, helmet, high-visibility jacket, goggles and ear-protectors in my locker, sign the book, and go home or on to the next thing. Five hours of careful conversation can be exhausting, but there is always a sense that something has happened, that connections have been made, that I've met someone new (and because of the five-shift pattern someone might be on the staff for a year before I meet them) – or that I have met with God, because, whether or not God's name has been mentioned, I have been with people made in God's image and have been in part of God's world and so a place where God's Spirit is at work. I say 'whether or not God's name has been mentioned', but I have often realized that there has been more God-talk during one visit to Tate & Lyle than during the whole of the previous week in the parish.

This is workplace chaplaincy. It isn't spectacular and it isn't easy, but it's an important component of the Church of England's ministry – and of the ministry of other denominations, for this is frequently an ecumenical ministry. It is carried out by clergy and by lay chaplains, and it is intimately connected with the Church's parishes, for it is often undertaken by clergy and others visiting the industry and commerce in their own parish.

## Industrial mission in south London

The work I do at the refinery is the way it all started. George Reindorp, the Rector of Woolwich, visited the deep shelters of Siemens Brothers, a large engineering company on the south bank of the Thames, during the blitz in 1942. When he became

Provost of Southwark Cathedral he invited Colin Cuttell to join the cathedral staff to visit the industries in the cathedral parish – and so the South London Industrial Mission (SLIM) was born. The strategy was always to gather a group in each factory and to recruit 'keymen' (yes, it was men) to organize events. Those were the days of the standard one-hour lunch-break, and there were discussions and lectures organized in works canteens, and there were talks in the apprentice schools. Those were also the days of the standard finishing-time, and people would leave work and attend a SLIM lecture or go on a weekend conference to the William Temple College in Rugby. There were publications and industry-based harvest thanksgiving services – but at the heart of it all was the team of chaplains, most of them parish priests, diligently visiting the industries in their parishes.

In Sheffield and elsewhere the approach was rather differ-ent. The vast steel mills often crossed parish boundaries, and their size meant that parish priests, often serving parishes with large populations, found the prospect rather daunting. So a team of full-time chaplains was recruited, and this is still the model in some parts of the country. In South London some of the industries were also large and had sites scattered across several parishes (such as the Electricity Generating Board), so SLIM too recruited a team of full-time chaplains. At its peak there was a team of a dozen, giving all or most of their time to industrial mission, with a large team of part-time chaplains, mainly parish priests, visiting smaller industrial sites.

Then, during the 1960s, London began to change. The large factories started to close and London's industries became small or medium-sized companies, shopping centres, local authorities, and the NHS. During the more secular 1970s it became difficult to negotiate new chaplaincies when old industries closed, so chaplains turned their attention to help-ing Christians in South London's churches to apply their faith to their work. When I joined the team in 1983 to work as an industrial chaplain in St Thomas's Hospital (yes, 'industrial' chaplain, because a teaching hospital is a large industry) and to extend the industrial chaplaincy model to the civil service, there were still chaplains but there were fewer chaplaincies. 'Issues' were the centre of attention in industrial missions up and down the country, and the denominations were beginning to wonder why they were paying for this. Where traditional chaplaincies remained the bedrock of activity, full-time or part-time (and increasingly part-time) chaplains remained the norm; but in London, where chaplaincies in the traditional industries had died out as the industries closed or moved, the new service and technology-based industries didn't provide the same scope for wandering round industrial sites or seeking opportunities for conversation, so decline set in. North of the river the Diocese of London closed down the London Industrial Chaplaincy, and south of the river the full-time posts slowly disappeared – leaving, by the 1990s, a handful of part-time chaplains visiting a handful of industries: one of which is Tate & Lyle's Greenwich Peninsula refinery. This is the last traditional industrial site on the south bank of the Thames, and it has one of the last industrial chaplains in London.

But that isn't the end of the story, because London is changing again, its institutions are diversifying, and chaplaincy to institutions is diversifying.

## A diversity of institutions

For eight years I have been chaplain of Westcombe Park Police Station. This is a small station and my chaplaincy consists of dropping in for an hour or so every now and then to listen to officers' concerns, to answer questions they put to me (and they do), and to debate issues in our community. This is where it gets a bit tricky, for my role is to be chaplain to police officers, but I am also a member of the community and a representative figure (see Chapter 16), so I might occasionally share some of the community's concerns about policing. It *is* possible to keep the roles separate, and sometimes I find myself inhabiting different roles within the same conversation.

I was also for a while chaplain to Greenwich Theatre – a real pleasure, because in theatre chaplaincy going to see the plays is both a responsibility and perk. Again, it was about meeting people: the staff when they were around, the company before the show.

Many police stations have chaplains, and most theatres do. This is chaplaincy to institutions, and if it sounded better then we'd call all of this work 'institutional chaplaincy'. That was what being one of the chaplains to the Millennium Dome was. During 2000 a team of 20 or so volunteers from a variety of churches were chaplains to both staff and visitors. We made ourselves available in the canteen, in the different themed zones, in the public spaces, and in the prayer space; we led public prayer twice a day; and we built relationships with members of other faiths. And chaplaincy to institutions is what the new multifaith chaplaincy to the Greenwich Peninsula is: though with this project we are entering a new chaplaincy world as the work will evolve through chaplaincy styles appropriate to the construction industry, to the new sports and music stadium, to the residents, to the leisure facilities, to the hotel, to the office blocks, and to new educational facilities. The evolution will occur by adding new institutions and not removing any, so the result will be a chaplaincy more diverse than any we have seen so far. The task will be the same: to be available, to listen, and to respond to institutions' and individuals' situations from within our religious tradition (in this case from within a diverse tradition); but here the institutional context will be diverse and evolving for the next 20 years, and probably beyond that.

LendLease, the main partner in the consortium building the Greenwich Peninsula development, also built Bluewater, a large retail complex outside Dartford. Here Malcolm Cooper is the chaplain: a full-time (Methodist) member of the Kent Industrial Mission team. His role is availability to staff, management, and customers; the co-ordination of a team of volunteer part-time chaplains to particular stores; and management of the multifaith prayer space, Q.

Retail is a growing industry, and chaplaincy to it is an expanding field. ASDA has actively sought chaplains for its stores, and in Charlton Jeffrey Heskins and his ecumenical colleagues are chaplains; and for a couple of years now Michael Dent, also on the staff of Kent Industrial Mission, has been recruiting volunteer chaplains, both clergy and laity, from among south London's churches, and placing them in retail and other industries. Training, supervision and support are offered, and chaplains can learn a lot from each other; but each chaplain is expected to evolve their own approach for each of them is in a unique situation, and each of them has their own gifts to offer. As Michael sees it, Jesus set people free to go and do wonderful things for the Kingdom of God. This is why he seeks volunteer chaplains: so that new things can be done for God's Kingdom in the institutions of their local economy.

This is the face of the new industrial mission. It is in one sense the old industrial mission, because it's the way it all started in south London: clergy and laity visiting workplaces in their parishes. But it is new because the institutions are different, and 'industry' isn't usually the right word. It's more accurate to call this 'mission in the economy' or 'workplace chaplaincy', and the person who does it a 'workplace chaplain'.

Michael has found, as I have, that sometimes you push a door and it doesn't open. Is this rejection a reaction to the Church's previous rejections of individuals in the company? Maybe. But, whatever the reason, some companies really don't want chaplains around. But some do, and some of today's new institutions do. Thus Fiona Stewart-Darling has been appointed Bishop's Chaplain in Docklands, for the workers at Canary Wharf, working in *all* of its many institutions: international banks and law firms, national newspapers, retail, and restaurants. This, like the Greenwich Peninsula Chaplaincy, takes a territory and plans chaplaincy to everything in it rather than being a chaplaincy to one type of institution. In this respect – apart from the fact that there is usually no gathered worshipping community – it is like parochial ministry, for that too, wherever possible, relates to whatever is there.

And then there's sports chaplaincy (Jeffrey Heskins is chaplain to Charlton Athletic Football Club, and we shall be glad of his expertise when the new stadium opens in the Millennium Dome); there is transport chaplaincy (for instance, there is a part-time chaplain to South Eastern Trains' headquarters offices in Croydon; and the London City Mission provides a number of transport chaplains); there is chaplaincy to local authorities, building on the long-standing tradition of mayors appointing chaplains; there are chaplains in schools (mainly in faith-based and private schools, but also in some others); and there are chaplains in prisons, hospitals and higher education establishments (usually in these cases paid by those institutions) – and the members of this last group get chapters of their own elsewhere in this book because these are distinctive ministries with characteristics all of their own.

So, while industrial mission, in the sense of chaplains visiting heavy manufacturing industry, might be in decline, chaplaincy to a wide diversity of institutions is alive and well; and alongside this development is a serious interest in the economy as a whole.

Andrew Wakefield is Vicar of St Andrew's, South Wimbledon, and there aren't many institutions in Merton's economy with which Andrew doesn't have some relationship. He's Chair of the Chamber of Commerce, a member of the Civic Partnership, and involved in a variety of other groups. In these roles he is both a representative of the Church and a local resident serving his community, and to this dual role he brings skills, contacts, and experience. Marcus Beale is a full-time architect, the Chair of the Civic Forum in Merton, and an active Christian and member of St Andrew's, South Wimbledon. Both the layperson and the priest are relating the Christian Faith to the institutions of our society and its economy and both of them enrich the Church as they communicate some of that experience. Similarly, in Croydon, Terry Drummond, a Church Army officer, runs or supports local institutions, and particularly skills agencies, and he is also Social Responsibility Officer for the Croydon Area of the Diocese of Southwark. He, like Marcus and Andrew, is exercising a ministry of connectedness, relating Christian and secular institutions to each other and thus tackling the institutional secularization that leads to an impoverished society and an impoverished Church.

And then of course there are the countless thousands of Christians living out their Christian faith in their places of work, trying to make a difference in a world in which no decisions are simple and in which we can only aim for the least evil solution to a problem and never the truly good one. Here is where costly discipleship happens: in the company employing accounting practices that are on the edge of integrity, in the electronics company with more and more of its orderbook related to armaments manufacture, and in the department store buying department where decisions are made about where to source the products to be sold. Some of these Christians will be Non-stipendiary Ministers and Ministers in Secular Employment (see Chapter 5). There is a case for deploying such ministers to those parishes or other institutions in the Church where their gifts and experience will have the greatest impact on the relationship between Christian faith and the economy and its institutions; and there is a strong case for better co-ordination between their work in the institutions of the economy and the work of workplace chaplains.

## Workplace chaplaincy in the twenty-first century

Both active involvement in our society's economic institutions and the pastoral care of Christians working in those institutions are legitimate and important tasks for a workplace chaplain, and they will be increasingly important as our economy and its institutions diversify. But the chaplain will do these tasks best if he or she continues diligently to visit industrial and commercial sites in order to be both pastor and prophet. These last sentences are not uncontentious. The Roman Catholic Church's attitude is that it's the laity who are the Church's representatives in places of work and that the priest's task is to care for the laity as they undertake this task. The Church of England's attitude, and that of most of the Free Churches, is that there is much to be gained from the ordained, representative person making themselves available within as well as outside the institutions of our society. Not only does this provide a clear and accessible focus for the Church's relationship to the institutional elements of our society, but it also informs the priest and thus enhances their ability to offer both pastoral care and prophecy among Christians.

The gospel is about each one of us as individuals, but the Kingdom of God which the gospel promises is a social reality – so just as it is the Church's responsibility to provide signposts for the individual to follow to enable the life of the Kingdom to be received as a gift and to be lived now, so we must provide signposts to the Kingdom within the economy as a whole and in all of its diverse institutions, for these too are called to reflect the grace-shaped Kingdom of God now, not just in the future or in the Kingdom when it fully comes.

So within these institutions both pastoral and prophetic ministry are required: pastoral ministry to express the generous love of God, and prophetic ministry to inspire the kind of change necessary to turn institutions (whether these be companies, other organizations, or such institutions as our tax and benefits system) into something closer in character to the Kingdom of God. The pastoral care is the chaplain's role, and the chaplain can sometimes fulfil a gently prophetic role too. Where a more abrasive prophecy is required the chaplain's role is to brief the churches with non-confidential information (and they might at the same time let the institutions to which they are chaplains know that they are doing this).

In London, moves towards a more diverse ministry to the economy and to its institutions are afoot. Traditional chaplaincy to institutions will continue to be part of this, and will itself be reinvigorated by the broader context; but there will be new approaches too as we find ways to be both pastoral and prophetic within the economy's institutions in all their diversity. We shall build on the long history of chaplains visiting industry, on the newer retail chaplaincies, and on the kind of work that Andrew Wakefield, Marcus Beale and Terry Drummond have been doing in Merton and Croydon: actively contributing to such institutions as training agencies, chambers of commerce and local partnerships and forums. And one of our tasks will be to seek new workplace chaplains among both the laity and the clergy of the Church (or rather, the churches, for workplace chaplaincy is one of those ministries that really ought to be conducted ecumenically); and we shall train them and support them: for workplace chaplaincy is no easy task.

Industrial chaplaincy and its younger siblings are perhaps the most difficult kinds of ministry. The chaplain to the workplace never belongs, they can be asked to leave tomorrow – no, today – and there are few maps. Every visit is a new experience. This can be both draining and exhilarating. It requires planning, reflection, supervision and training. (The Industrial Mission Association provides good initial training, and some industrial missions provide supervision and continuing training, but more is needed, particularly for the increasing number of very part-time chaplains.) In London and in other places a good deal more co-ordination would be useful too. There *is* a lot of good work being done by Christians in the institutions in which they work, by organizations that research and debate issues, and by congregations relating to local institutions: but little information passes between these activities, and in many cases people doing them feel isolated and unsupported. Opportunities for conversation is the primary requirement.

Above all we need to *do* it. We need to relate practically to institutions. It often starts with tenuous links – a phone call, a Christmas card. And then the building of relationships, then an experiment, then a regular commitment, with agreements eventually formalized on confidentiality, insurance, health and safety training and clothing, accountability, and regularity of visits.

For some contexts and for some individuals full-time chaplaincy will be right, and the churches together (and other faiths too) will need to provide for this; but recent changes in the nature of industry and commerce mean that in the future the norm will be part-time chaplains, often offering only a few hours a month. Such chaplains need to be recruited, trained, placed, and supervised, and anyone either in or considering ministry in the Church, of whatever kind, ought to be considering whether some of their time ought to be given to ministry in the economy and in economic and social institutions.

It is perhaps the hardest and the most rewarding ministry there is.

## Further reading

Board for Social Responsibility of the General Synod of the Church of England, *Industrial Mission: An Appraisal*, Church House Publishing, London, 1988.
www.industrialmission.org

# 13. Serving in a Walled Community
## The Prison Chaplain

### ALISON TYLER

I came to the exiles . . . And I sat there among them. (Ezekiel 3.15)

## The prison and the prisoners

At first glance the prison has many of the characteristics of a parish: a defined community, a place of worship, a priest, and a regularly worshipping community. But a moment's reflection indicates that the similarities are superficial and that prison ministry is like no other, though it might have a few common characteristics with hospitals, boarding schools and monasteries. The prison community is a captive, compelled community; there is no voluntary membership. Not only that, those in prison are compelled to live in unnaturally close proximity with a large number of strangers, some of whom may be dangerous, many of whom will be vulnerable or mentally ill, and none of whom they were able to choose. This is by itself a stressful experience.

Prison ministry differs from parish work in a number of key ways. There are few infant baptisms or marriages, except among the staff. I am not licensed to perform weddings, nor is the chapel licensed to hold them. We visit the sick, either in the healthcare centre or in hospital, and we conduct funerals, but not many, except for staff or for prisoners who have no families or next of kin. There is no Parochial Church Council, but there are a lot of other meetings. There are also good employment conditions, and proper time off.

A prison is a hierarchical, structured organization, a secular community, in social and political terms a public service, and often a political hot potato. Currently there are 74–75,000 people in prison at any one time; some 4,000+ are women and some 6,000+ are in maximum security establishments. So the need for chaplains is unlikely to diminish.

Members of prison communities are unlike those in the average parish. There is a wealth of literature (see further reading) illustrating the fact that, by every measure of disadvantage, our prisoners score very highly. Prisoners include disproportionately high numbers of the mentally ill, those suffering from depression, adults who were children in care or from broken homes, the educationally deprived (either with learning difficulties, or through truanting, or due to frequent moves), substance abusers, those who have themselves been physically or sexually abused, and those who have recognizable but untreatable personality disorders. A recent series of articles in the *Guardian* (December 2004) focused on the mental health needs of prisoners. There is insufficient provision for the mentally ill, who may end up offending and thus going to prison because there is nowhere else for them to go.

There are also disproportionate numbers of people from minority ethnic groups in prison, not all of them British. Where I work 44 per cent of the prisoners are currently foreign nationals. To be a stranger in a strange land and in prison is the worst of all possible prison situations; there are the extra problems of no one to talk to in your own language, and difficulty in contacting family, friends and home, on top of all the usual constraints and problems of just being in prison. There is also the shame of setting off to make some much-needed money, and then being arrested at the airport, convicted, sentenced and, when deported at the end of your sentence, having in some countries to serve your sentence again as a punishment for bringing your nation into disrepute. It was George who, at the end of such a sentence and facing that prospect, said to me in response to my question 'Will it be difficult to be going home?', 'Oh no, I am happy every day because of my salvation, there is joy in my heart every day because God has done so much for me.' I never heard that said in a parish – even on a good day.

People in prison are much more likely to practise their faith than those outside; about 600 of our 1,200 prisoners are likely to attend some form of worship in a week, and only about one in six say that they have no religion. It is something to do with reaching rock bottom, and needing every possible resource with which to continue to survive, and this may mean revisiting childhood faith or discovering faith for the first time, and clinging on to it. One of my colleagues pointed out to me that *The Message* Bible translation of Lamentations 3 (p.1115) sums it up completely (especially for the drug user):

> I'll never forget the trouble, the utter lostness,
> The taste of ashes, the poison I've swallowed.
> I remember it all – oh how well I remember –
> The feeling of hitting the bottom.
> But there's one other thing I remember,
> And remembering, I keep a grip on hope.
>
> God's loyal love couldn't have run out,
> His merciful love couldn't have dried up.
> They're created new every morning.
> How great your faithfulness!
> I'm sticking with God (I say it over and over),
> He's all I've got left.

When I walk round the prison people often come up and ask for a blessing, as a reassurance and a remembrance that God, who knows their name, does not forget them, and has it written on the palm of his hand. I am sure that this is because prison is a very stripped down environment, with little in the way of individual recognition. It will generally be a single-sex community, men or women of similar age living in tightly packed communities, with no children, few old people, in cramped conditions and largely powerless to control the structure of their days. There is all that is needed to maintain life, but little to encourage individualism, self-expression, or 'whole person flourishing', and despite the best efforts of the prison service, people in prison spend a lot of their time locked up.

Those of us who come from parish life to minister in prison are used to people having problems, but mostly able to deal with them with a little help, and to live generally self-directed lives. It is a shock to see how much power is lost by imprisonment: there is no possibility of controlling or influencing what goes on outside among friends, family and community. Contact is by letter, phone or visit, all of which are in short supply due to the logistical problems of providing those opportunities even-handedly and in sufficient quantity for the numbers in the overcrowded prison system. Being locked in under someone else's control means complete loss of freedom of movement and an inability to make many decisions for yourself – and any that are made can only be put into effect with someone else's help. There is also the endless noise, infinite varieties of other people's music, the clanging of gates, the rattling of keys, the shouting, the bells, and the buzzers.

If someone you love becomes terminally ill while you are in prison, provided they are a close enough relative, you can be taken to visit them. However, it takes time to arrange, checks have to be made to make sure they really are ill and likely to die, staff have to be detailed to take you there, travel has to be arranged, and often by the time it has been set up the person has died. Then the whole process has to be done again to get the prisoner to the funeral, often under escort and also with handcuffs. This turns a family bereavement into a potential nightmare. A father said to me that he did not want his son to come to his mother's funeral, as no one else knew his son was in prison and he could not stand the shame of it being known in the family. Fortunately the prisoner was released in time to attend as a free man, but this is not always the case.

There is a great deal of bereavement and grief, for the lives that prisoners have not been able to live because of the circumstances of their childhoods, for the family relationships disrupted by imprisonment, for the children or parents who they lose contact with, for the efforts that they have made which have come to nothing, and for their friends and relatives who die of overdoses and in accidents. I find myself in complete agreement with those of my colleagues who are convinced that many of our prisoners who abuse alcohol and drugs do so as a form of self-medication to deaden the pain of their lives. It certainly seems to delay it. One colleague tells of the man who asked for help dealing with a bereavement some seven years previously, which he said was as painful as if it had happened yesterday. This was because he had been using heroin ever since the death and had not had any time for the grieving. Now that he was clean he could feel the pain and needed to do the work.

Some prisoners do manage to maintain strong and positive attitudes, to maintain their links with family and friends, to take every opportunity to improve their skills, to meet and to pray, and to plan for their own future after prison. One man who I knew in a London prison said to me: 'Alison, I see it like this, a prison is like a monastery; I don't see myself as locked in, I see the world as locked out, so that I have the time, free from distractions, to think, to pray and to learn more about myself . . . and God.' He is a rare person. He gave up his television during Lent and never asked for it back because it was a distraction, and he takes full responsibility for his own behaviour and is determined that the future will be different, better, and free from crime.

There is much pain involved in being a prisoner. Events such as bereavement, difficult under any circumstances, become much worse because of the isolation, the difficulty of contact, and the inability to initiate action. There is also a great deal of waiting – for news, to be unlocked, to get on to a course or into a class, for meals, for exercise, for a visit, for conviction and sentence, for transfer, for a decision to be made and above all for release. Waiting begets frustration, impatience, tension, and potentially violence or self-harm. Much of the energy of the chaplains is used in sitting with prisoners in their distress, in the dark times, perhaps in the aftermath of violence or bullying, in situations in which nothing can be done but listen and pray quietly for God's blessing of peace, healing and wholeness for the man or woman concerned. It is very important to listen and really hear what is being said, and to try and keep hope alive in such situations, because when hope is lost people are most vulnerable to attempts at self-harm or suicide.

## The chaplain

The prison chaplain today is a member of a faith community, licensed or accredited by that community to minister to the religious, spiritual and pastoral needs of prisoners and staff in the prison to which they are appointed. We operate according to the Prison Service Standards on Religion, which are, like all prison standards, auditable. The prison setting is a very stressful workplace, as well as being an extremely difficult experience for those who are imprisoned in it. The chaplain always used to be an Anglican, and no prison could open without an Anglican chaplain. Other Christian chaplains, and then other faith chaplains, were appointed on the basis of need to minister to the different faith groups in individual prisons. Now there are full-time chaplains who are Church of England, Roman Catholic, Free Church and Muslim. There are as many different kinds of chaplain as there are prisoners. The chaplaincy in a large prison is a multi-faith team, managed by either a competent chaplain or a governor.

We are employed by the prison service, interviewed and appointed by recruitment boards, and paid as civil servants. It sounds more like a secular job than a religious vocation. Having said that, it is such a specialized form of ministry that few would undertake it if it were not something to which they believed they were called by God and the Church. It is an enormous privilege to be able to minister in the prison setting, though it is fraught with frustration, difficulty, and massive feelings of impotence when confronted by the quantity of need, hope and aspiration into which we are invited to pour our energies.

The Church of England chaplain is licensed by the diocesan bishop as well as appointed by the prison service, and they both hold the chaplain accountable for different aspects of the job. This creates the potential for conflicts of interest, which fortunately seldom materialize.

I have been a chaplain since 1998, and have worked at Her Majesty's Prison (HMP) Brixton, Her Majesty's Young Offenders Institution (HMYOI) Feltham, HMP Wandsworth and, since July 2002, at HMP Wormwood Scrubs. Before I was a chaplain I was a probation officer, but some years after I was ordained three different people said to me in consecutive weeks that they were expecting to hear that I had become a prison chaplain; in the fourth week there was an advert in the *Church Times*, and I applied.

Many of the things that the chaplain does in a prison are intangible and do not have measurable outcomes, so cannot be quantified. Thus we have to find ways to measure our work and to demonstrate that we are value for money. On the other hand, merely by being in the prison we are stating that 'this is not all there is, there is more', and by celebrating the Eucharist in such a hierarchical organization we are being subversive, proclaiming by that egalitarian foretaste of the heavenly banquet that all are equal before God.

Chaplains are an integral part of the prison. Some are on the senior management teams of their establishments, and all of us are involved in the various groups and committees that co-ordinate the work of the prison. These include groups relating to suicide and self-harm, violence reduction, drug strategy and public protection, anti-bullying, security, training, race relations and diversity, and resettlement. One of my colleagues runs the staff care team of staff volunteers who provide support for their colleagues who have been involved in serious incidents like assaults or suicide. The suicide rates among both staff and prisoners cause much concern both inside and outside the prison service.

Contrary to the impression often given in the media, when someone dies or kills themselves in a prison the staff who care for them are always distressed, often deeply shocked, and usually in need of care and support themselves. Sadly, among the prisoners, the ones who kill themselves are often those who have given no prior indication of their intent, or are those who intend a cry for help and hope to be discovered in time. Unfortunately they are not always found alive.

In our multi-faith team the Christian chaplains seek not only to be Christ for the community but also, with the others, to model collaborative working among the faiths, races and genders. Chaplains are not allowed to evangelize or to proselytize, or actively to seek converts to our faiths. We are there to fulfil the needs of those who ask. It is an interesting mix and balance of the spiritual, the pastoral, and the politically correct.

## The working day

There is no such thing as a typical day in a prison, although our days do have certain common features. I can make plans for the work, but they are almost invariably overturned by the happenings of the day. I may fail to show up at meetings and social engagements because something has happened in the prison that prevents me from leaving. The basic shape of the day involves one of us attending the governor's morning meeting with the function heads, and exchanging the news of the main events of the past day and plans for the new day. We share this information with colleagues, have brief prayers together if possible, and then move on to work in the prison.

We see the new receptions (those who were sent by the courts in the preceding 24 hours), visit the wings, see those who have asked us to visit, and visit the healthcare centre and also the Segregation (or Care and Control) Unit where those who need to be kept separately for reasons of safety or discipline are held. There will then be meetings of various kinds, and then visitors: official prison visitors, official visitors (including those who come from overseas to see what a British prison is like), and those who want to become volunteers. (Prison chaplaincy attracts both the most committed and the least suitable people among those who volunteer, so they have to be carefully selected and trained.) Almost every day we have meetings to do with sentence planning, or suicide prevention. Those who are assessed as being at risk of self-harm are reviewed regularly by a multi-disciplinary team on their wings, and plans are made to try and build up their ability to cope, or to alleviate their distress. Several of my colleagues see all those who are registered as being at risk of self-harm at least once a week.

We are often the ones who break bad news to prisoners. In fact, the ability to break bad news is a core competence for chaplains. It can be a time-consuming and distressing task because we have to confirm the news, which is usually about a death or serious illness, and hospitals and doctors do not always want to tell us as we are not family members. Sadly people sometimes phone to say that someone has died in order to cause distress to someone against whom they have a grudge. It is this kind of situation that has led to the system of checks and enquiries. My worst ever day at work was one on which I had to confirm the deaths of five people, and then tell the five prisoners that someone they loved had died. It is not always bad news. We often have to tell people that they have become fathers (although on occasion this may also be bad news), but the good news is always dulled by the fact of being unable to share the experience or see the baby.

In our team there are a lot of us – full-time, part-time, volunteers and sessional colleagues – and so we have to meet regularly. Those of us who are full-time at Wormwood Scrubs try to meet together weekly, and as a whole team we meet at least quarterly. We have to plan our work for the year, review our budget annually and, if we need more resources, make a business case to submit for them.

We provide a variety of religious activity and religious education for prisoners. We run a range of Bible study groups, Islamic classes and meditation opportunities. We also run an Alpha course, courtesy of some wonderful volunteers and the Alpha for Prisons team. The prison service as a whole has the task of addressing offending behaviour, and as part of that programme we facilitate the running of the Sycamore Tree course on Victim Awareness by the Prison Fellowship group. Again they are volunteers, and they make a large contribution to the work of the chaplaincy. The Sycamore Tree course enables prisoners to consider and experience the impact of their crime on their victims. It has been shown that once you see the potential victim as a real, or whole, person it is more difficult to target them. It also challenges people to take responsibility for their own actions in the future so that they will no longer be able to say 'I didn't know what I was doing'.

## The worshipping week

There is a variety of worship in our prison every day. There are our own daily prayers. On Mondays we have Sikh prayers, on Wednesdays Buddhist meditation, on Thursdays Hindu prayers, on Fridays Muslim prayers, on Saturdays Roman Catholic Mass and confession, and on Sundays two Roman Catholic Masses and two Church of England services. The Church of England services are open to everyone, although for the others you need to be registered as a member of the faith concerned, or a recognized enquirer, in order to attend.

Church of England services cater for all non-Roman Catholic Christians, so we have a wide variety of visiting church groups on a Sunday, from Pentecostal to Seventh Day Adventist. I actively discourage those who come to preach only hellfire and damnation, opting for those who will preach the unconditional love of God, because I believe that, once you are convinced of that love you will pass judgement on your own sins and discover your own need for repentance as a response to God's love, rather than having it forced upon you. But visitors come only on alternate Sundays because those of us who carry the misery during the week firmly believe that we are responsible for laying it before God on Sunday and that we need to do it often.

I give communion to whoever comes, and I know that I have shared the body of Christ with Sikhs, Muslims, Jews and Hindus. In a prison, where everyone has already been judged and found wanting by society, I cannot in all conscience deny the Sacrament to anyone who asks for it. It is particularly moving to give communion to those in prison because for that brief time they feel that they are no longer prisoners but full members of the wider Christian family. Many of the men say in response not 'Amen' but 'Thank you' on receiving the Sacrament. It is a very different experience from administering communion outside the prison.

On Thursdays those of us who are in the prison and are Anglican (some two or three), and sometimes one or two other Christian staff, share in a Eucharist together in order to put ourselves before God and renew our own commitment and energy.

Prison worship is great fun. If you preach something that the prisoners agree with then they will sometimes join in with 'yes' and fervent 'A-mens', but if you pray for something they don't approve of you may hear 'Oh f*** off Miss' from somewhere near the back. The prisoners greatly appreciate variety in worship, but this is coupled with a need for continuity and support. Prisoners often experience the prison regime both as boring and as inconsistent and unpredictable, and therefore seem to like worship to be both interesting and reliable. The supreme compliment for me was to be told by a prisoner, after one very spectacular set of Sunday visitors. 'It's all very well for them to come here and show off on Sunday, but you are always here on Monday.'

My observation is that even those unused to formal patterns of worship value and appreciate it when it is presented with conviction and flexibility.

As a woman priest in a men's prison I often find myself being the only woman present at Sunday worship, and male colleagues in women's prisons may find themselves in a similar situation; but it generally seems to make no difference to the quality of the response, and none of the prisoners has ever commented on it, either positively or negatively. The important thing for me is this: where else would one get the chance to share the Word of God with 120+ men on a Sunday morning? The important thing for the prisoners must surely be that, when they were in prison 'we' visited them, we sat where they sit, and who 'we' are is mostly irrelevant as long as we are there for them.

## Reflection

Those of us who work in prison chaplaincy tend to believe that we are not just on the cutting edge of ministry, but on the bleeding edge, dealing daily with things that are of real and pressing concern to people who have no other resources. We are doing this in the most diverse of communities, under great stress, and in great distress. It is a very extreme environment, complete with rats, rubbish, cockroaches, sometimes violence, and often pain; and it is extreme in terms of constraint and restriction, for both prisoners and staff. When reported in the media, prisons and their staff attract universal opprobrium, particularly when things go wrong or people die. In all walks of life there are those who behave badly, and prison is no different. In all the prisons I have known I have been continually impressed by the work of prison staff and by their high levels of care, commitment and professionalism under extremely trying circumstances.

It is difficult to reflect briefly on such an incoherent and busy working situation. However, Ezekiel's notion of sitting with those in captivity contains within it a wealth of possibility, and fulfils one of the fundamental criteria of priesthood: that of being, rather than doing. We are those who pray for healing for God's people, celebrate the sacraments with them, offer them companionship on a difficult road, offer God's blessing, and encourage repentance, with the assurance of sins forgiven to those who are in distress. It is impossible to read the Ordinal and not to believe that this ministry is one of those places where God wants priests, not just social workers. As Paul says in 2 Corinthians 5.14, 'The love of Christ urges us on . . .' Both clergy and laity alike experience prison ministry as a compulsion.

Prison ministry totally affirms the 'mission statement' of Isaiah 61.1–3a:

> The spirit of the Lord God is upon me,
> because the Lord has anointed me;
> he has sent me to bring good news to the oppressed,
> to bind up the broken-hearted,
> to proclaim liberty to the captives,
> and release to the prisoners;
> to proclaim the year of the Lord's favour,
> and the day of vengeance of our God;
> to comfort all who mourn;
> to provide for those who mourn in Zion –
> to give them a garland instead of ashes,
> the oil of gladness instead of mourning,
> the mantle of praise instead of a faint spirit.

Prisoners come into all the categories: oppressed, broken-hearted, captive, in prison, and in mourning. Of all people, they are among those who most need to hear 'good news'.

Prisons are often in the news in ways that, as the Bishop for Prisons Peter Selby said recently, reflect our ambivalence about crime and criminals. As a society we worry about crime and we want those who commit it dealt with; but we cannot decide whether we want them punished or reconciled, and nor do we seem able to develop strategies for keeping people out of prison or for settling them back into the community after they leave prison. And there are those prisoners for whom prison is a place of respite and safety, and who really do want to be there. We need to ask questions about what kind of society we have made that it is so difficult to live in that some people can't. The reality is that the world's worst criminals are not in prison. They are the successful ones who thrive on the misery and deaths of others, who seek to corrupt and undermine morality in society, who interfere with the democratic processes, and who become rich and powerful as they do so. Those who end up with us in prison are those who are often already poor, outcast and marginalized. By the time many of them come here, every other social agency has already failed them: family, school, social services and probation.

I am writing this in the weeks before Christmas, and already we are looking forward to celebrating (really!) another Christmas behind bars. The prison Alpha group in the Scrubs have written a carol that begins 'It's Christmas time, even at Wormwood Scrubs'.

In the rare quiet moments that sometimes occur when walking round the prison on dark evenings, I do find myself thanking God for sending me here, and entrusting me with this somewhat precarious and difficult ministry for a while. When the bishop gives the chaplain the licence, he gives the chaplain to the prison as a rather strange form of gift to be unpacked and explored at leisure and as needed. No two of us are the same and neither are the places within which we minister.

## Further reading

Gorringe, T. J., *Crime*, in the series Changing Society and the Churches, SPCK, London, 2004.

Jones, C. and Sedgwick, P. (eds), *The Future of Criminal Justice – Resettlement, Chaplaincy and Community*, SPCK, London, 2002.

Board of Social Responsibility, *Prisons: A Study in Vulnerability*, Church House Publishing, London, 1999.

Catholic Bishops Conference, *A Place of Redemption: A Christian Approach to Punishment and Prison*, Burns & Oates, London, 2004.

# 14. Serving in a Learning Community
## The Chaplain in Higher Education

### PAUL COLLIER

The beginning of wisdom is this: Get wisdom,
   and whatever else you get, get insight.
Prize her highly, and she will exalt you;
   she will honour you if you embrace her.
She will place on your head a fair garland;
   shewill bestow on you a beautiful crown.
(Proverbs 4.7–9)

When in 2002 I decided to move from parish ministry into higher education chaplaincy, I was looking forward to being in an academic environment among people who enjoyed thinking critically in ways that would test my theology. I was also looking forward to finding out how the Christian message related to an age group (18–25) that was largely absent from the inner-city parishes where I had served. I have not been disappointed. But I had not been prepared for the radically different shape of higher education ministry, nor had I anticipated how disorientating it is not to have a gathered community to serve and be part of, and not to have Sunday morning as the focal point of my working week. Now that I have been just over two years in my new post I am coming to terms with what is in many ways a very marginal role in a large institution. I recognize that two years is not long, and Goldsmiths College, being part of the federal University of London, is very different from campus universities and from places like Oxford and Cambridge, but I have been able to draw some initial conclusions that might be of interest.

Licensed in January 2003 as Anglican Chaplain at Gold-smiths College I found myself with something of a blank canvas on which to create a role. The Diocese of Southwark had begun to withdraw from the chaplaincy at Goldsmiths many years previously, and had sold the chaplaincy building, so that all that was left for me to inherit three years after the previous chaplain had left was a free-standing, half-time post with no accommodation. In these circumstances, Gold-smiths, as a secular institution, had been offered little reason to question a view of religion as either irrelevant or dangerous in the context of the education and personal development of its students. Fortunately for me other factors had started to come into play, and particularly some key changes in person-nel and a rise in the importance of student services in higher education. By the time of my appointment the College was prepared to see provision made for the religious needs of students and staff, and was willing to contribute by provid-ing a chaplaincy office. There was an expectation that there would be no intrusive or aggressive proselytizing, and a posi-tive expectation that the chaplain would work ecumenically and with faith communities other than their own. (A report prepared for General Synod on Higher Education and Further Education Chaplaincy, entitled *Pillars of the Church,* revealed that in the Church there was often little grasp of what higher education chaplaincy is about, other than an erroneous belief left over from a bygone era that higher education institutions provide fertile ground for vocations.)

While there was little understanding of chaplaincy in either the Church or the College, I was fortunate to have as my line manager in the student services department a com-mitted Anglican who was an active churchgoer in one of the Diocese of Southwark's largest evangelical congregations. Although with a very different churchmanship to my own, Helen McNeely was an invaluable support as someone who understood the values and language of faith, but also knew the College well and understood its ethos and structures. We were clear that the chaplaincy could not be an evangelistic outpost in higher education seeking conversions to the Christian faith, but exactly what shape of ministry might be worthwhile, within the particular ethos and context of Goldsmiths, would have to be discovered by trial and error.

## The role of chaplaincy

Making use of the existing support networks for London chaplaincies, and in particular receiving excellent help and advice from the National Higher Education adviser at Church House, Hugh Shilson-Thomas, a pattern for chaplaincy work emerged. Most chaplaincies find that there are three strands to their work, which may be described as being a 'friend' to the institution, providing pastoral care to students and staff, and presenting the challenge of faith. Although some chaplains have done very effective work by concentrating their energy in one of these areas, most find a more even balance. How would it work out for me at Goldsmiths?

### A friend to the institution

My own experience of school and university had led me to take for granted the access given to the Church of England by our major institutions. We expect the voice of the Church to be heard and respected, and we expect to be treated as natural partners to the secular institutions that make up our national life: schools, hospitals and prisons. Because this position has been established over many centuries we have little realization of how easily this ground can be lost and how hard it is to win it back. At Goldsmiths I expected the chaplain to be treated as a natural ally in the educational endeavour, and as someone who could be called on to make a valuable contribution to the institutional structures. Although my presence was not unwelcome, I quickly came to realize that as chaplain I was not actually viewed as belonging to the College at all, but rather as a bolt-on service provided for a small minority of students. Two stories may serve as illustrations.

I had decided at the outset to wear clerical dress in the college in order to be a visible presence. While it served to get me noticed, there was also a more negative impact. One senior tutor whom I met for lunch as a way of introducing myself was noticeably alarmed by my arrival in clerical collar. At the time I dismissed this attitude as over-sensitivity in the person concerned. Later I came to realize how in an academic environment it could be seen as a confrontational statement: a challenge to a secular ethos. Whereas I intended to represent the Church as an ally of the educational enterprise, it was possible also to interpret my clerical dress as a signal that I sought to change the whole ethos of the college by establishing a visible religious presence.

My second story is a subtle illustration from the opposite perspective. When, sadly, the warden (equivalent to a vice-chancellor) died in 2004, I was surprised not to be given the responsibility for organizing the memorial service, which was held at the college later in the year. I realized, however, that this was another example of the chaplain not being seen as part of the College, but only as a religious person allowed to function within the College. Instead, a college committee was formed to organize the service, including me as a member of the committee to advise on the religious dimension. It worked very well, but in a subtle way also underlined my place in the College.

It is perhaps obvious that for any secular institution to trust a chaplain to preserve and promote its own ethos there needs first to be long-term experience of the chaplain actively supporting that ethos. A member of staff from the Internal Communications Department recently confirmed to me that whereas she had thought of the chaplain very much as being relevant only to religious people, she could now see how I could contribute to the life of the College as a whole. The kind of presence in university life that chaplains can provide requires continuity, and it is quickly dissipated if the Church's commitment to chaplaincy is seen to be intermittent or less than wholehearted, or as coming with a hidden agenda. In this respect the chaplain in a university is not so much like the priest in a parish, but rather like the parish church in relation to the parish as a whole. The church has to get involved in the life of the local community in order to earn the respect and interest of local people. The difference for a chaplain is that without all the preparation and activity involved in Sunday morning worship there is nothing that hides from us our lack of relevance to the community around us.

## A pastor to all

A more immediately obvious-seeming role for a chaplain is that of offering pastoral care to all of the college's students and staff. Here, too, there is a clear need for a sense of trust to be established within the institution before the chaplain's role will begin to be as effective as it can be. Moreover, with the high turnover of students (the vast majority moving on after three years) there is a second stage to the process: chaplains have to be trusted by *staff* to exercise an appropriate and valuable pastoral role with students before staff will point students in our direction. Again, a consistent history is the key factor. Recently I mentioned to a member of the senior management team that I didn't feel that students' personal tutors could be suggesting the chaplaincy as a source of pastoral care. The response I received was that if they knew that I was going to be around for six or seven years then personal tutors might see me as part of the pattern of pastoral care in the College. It was an off-the-cuff remark, but rather a telling one.

Apart from the needs that arise in all sections of the population for care and counselling at times of crisis and stress, most students in higher education are experiencing a time of profound change as they develop towards mature adulthood, and they can benefit hugely from good pastoral care – a factor, no doubt, in the Government's requirement for every student to be offered the opportunity to discuss a personal development plan with their tutor. I remember when I first arrived at Goldsmiths being struck by the paradoxical combination in many students of confidence in their own abilities and independence and at the same time considerable vulnerability.

Chaplains, like parochial clergy, have their share of stories of dramatic pastoral interventions, where the opportunity to be alongside people at times of crisis and tragedy has been intensely moving and sometimes life-changing for those involved. My own experience at Goldsmiths has been of more commonplace times of difficulty dealing with bereavement, relationship problems, and issues of faith and belief. However, a research project carried out at a campus university in the north of England has provided a fascinating insight into an important area of students' pastoral care. It has the potential to affect not only the impact of chaplaincy on individual students, but also, if the resources were available, for chaplaincy to make a hugely significant contribution to university life.

The study found that for the vast majority of students who went straight to university from school, their number one priority during their time there – higher in importance than academic achievement and future career prospects – was the formation of their personal identity. In practice this process tended to manifest itself in the taking on of one of a number of possible group identities: punk, goth, sporty, arty, etc. Belonging to the group determines how you dress, the pubs and clubs where you hang out, and so on, and it is normally accompanied by considerable antipathy to those outside your group. The methodology of the study was the use of volunteers to engage in regular reflection with the researcher on a one-to-one basis on the experience of being a student. Interestingly for our purposes, the process of reflecting on their behaviour led many of the participants to obtain a more objective insight into their behaviour than was possible while in their group. This often included recognizing patterns of behaviour that were determined by group mentality and scapegoating rather than being a reflection of their own values: so when a student described how one flatmate had been excluded by the others for not belonging to the 'right' crowd he recognized what a 'naff' way it was to behave. In this way, someone with time to listen was found to have made a significant contribution to the student's growth in maturity.

With the pressure on higher education institutions to cater for larger numbers of students, the time that tutors are able to devote to non-academic aspects of student life is ever-diminishing. At the same time the needs of students are increasing as greater numbers come from backgrounds with little knowledge or expectation of higher education. Well-resourced chaplaincy, operating with the explicit support of the higher education institutions, could make a real difference.

### Presenting the challenge of faith

This third area of a chaplain's role involves the things that most people assume the job is all about: supporting those who are already active participants in their faith tradition, and offering opportunities to explore questions of faith with those who are not committed. It is with this picture in mind that many people wonder how I fill my time in such a secular environment as Goldsmiths is thought (largely accurately) to be. In truth, the response to what the chaplaincy offers in this regard can often seem very meagre compared to the effort that goes into it. One of my early bright ideas at the beginning of 2003, as the British Government was gearing up for the war in Iraq, was to organize a service of multi-faith prayers for peace. The non-religious were pleased to see that such an event was taking place, but few wanted to take part themselves. By contrast, most of the religiously minded, including the Islamic Society and the Christian Union, were too uncomfortable with the idea of multi-faith prayers to want to take part either. Of the half-dozen or so who turned up, four were students in the Media and Communications Department who wanted to get some material for a project for their course.

The London-based higher education institutions are at a particular disadvantage when it comes to extra-curricular activities, as students may live quite long distances away, and/ or have significant continuing family commitments. Many students have lectures and seminars on only three days a week, and there is rarely a day and time for an event that is convenient for more than a fraction of students at any one time. What produces an encouraging response one term may never get off the ground during another. A colleague had a lively group of first- and second-year students meeting for discussion regularly on Monday evenings. Excited by the success of the group, the following term he organized a varied programme of talks, discussions and outings, only to discover that many could no longer come on Mondays because of timetable changes, and without a critical mass the group disintegrated. His carefully prepared programme had to be cancelled. Flexibility and trial and error are the name of the game, and you've got to keep trying if you want a few things to work.

There is a particular difficulty here in the early years of establishing a chaplaincy. There is much to be said for an 'inside-out' model of ministry – that is, going out from inside the faith community to meet other people, rather than seeking to bring people in from outside – but there is a difficulty if having met people outside there is nothing to invite people to come and belong to. If you meet people in ones and twos, how are you ever going to achieve a critical mass of students who form a sufficiently large group to be attractive to potential newcomers?

A model that the evangelical Christian tradition has found particularly fruitful, but which has been largely left untried by others, is that of developing strong and lively student-centred worship and activities in a nearby parish church. All Saints, Peckham, for instance, has for many years attracted a significant number of Goldsmiths students, mainly those who belong to the Christian Union. This does not happen by accident. A great deal of energy and lots of resources have been put in over many years to create at All Saints a congregation and an atmosphere of worship that students can relate to. At the same time, huge resources of energy and time are also expended each year in making sure that as many students as possible are aware that there is a local church at which they will find a genuine welcome. Many students do take up the opportunity to find out what it is all about, and many stay. If those of us who believe in a more open, inclusive, and questioning approach to faith put in the same kind of resources, the results could also be dramatic. And we could avoid the impression being created that Christianity only exists in an evangelical package.

Opportunities to present the challenges of faith are often scarce, and they take the form of scattering seeds that may lie dormant for many years before there is an opportunity for further exploration. What is important is establishing a visible presence. Another colleague from a different university has told me of receiving a letter from a newly graduated student who wrote, 'You don't know me, but you were a great support to a friend of mine, and just knowing that you would help me if I needed you has contributed to me getting through my degree.'

## The demands of chaplaincy

I have shown, I hope, how different the role of a higher education chaplain is to that of a parish priest. Inevitably this means that the demands of the role are very different, too. In fact, the whole pattern of ministry is different, working to a different rhythm week by week, working at the margins rather than at the centre of an institution, and working in isolation rather than at the centre of a worshipping community.

## Working to different rhythms

There are several ways in which the rhythm of ministry in higher education chaplaincy is different from the rhythm of parish life. One of the most difficult things to adjust to in such chaplaincy has been the fact that the pattern of ministry does not centre on a weekly gathering of the faithful. In parish life, whatever else happens in a given week, however productive or unproductive a priest feels, and however successful or not particular events may have been, there is usually a predictable level of attendance at the main Sunday service, and with it a sense of the priest's main task having been adequately discharged. In higher education chaplaincy this focus very often does not exist, and it is possible to feel engaged in little effective activity. The gleanings are often small and thinly spread – two or three at morning prayer, half a dozen at a discussion group, a couple of meaningful conversations at the student union bar. There is no single weekly event that can be said to be my main task and on which I may concentrate my efforts. This problem is compounded by the fact that the academic year leaves out the principal festivals of Christmas and Easter. Such Christian community as there is disappears at the times of year most significant to us as Christians. Contrast the Islamic Society who can expect to double their numbers for the season of Ramadan.

One significant consequence of this pattern is that it is easy to neglect one's own spiritual disciplines and relationship with God. Here, too, there is potential for a creative partnership between chaplaincy and parish. One of the most sustaining things for me has been a weekly ecumenical morning prayer in the local deanery, where the support and interest of local parochial clergy has been something of a life-saver.

The academic year also has its own rhythm, with a concentration of activity in the first two terms. In the third term the focus is almost entirely on revision and exams, and there is little time or energy for engagement with other matters. I have consequently been learning the importance of using the period from May to September as a time for planning,

administration, writing and preparation. The more advance
work that I can do in terms of updating information, web-
page design, planning events, designing posters and so on, the
more I can be a presence out and about in the College in the
crucial period of September to April.

Finally the cycle of chaplaincy work in the 'inside-out'
model requires a response to a student-centred rather than a
chaplaincy-led agenda. Not much happens by deciding what I
think the chaplaincy programme should be and then trying to
implement it by trying to attract people to what I am offering.
Rather, I have to find out what students seem to be responding to and then try to provide it. Interestingly, of the initiatives I have attempted in the last two years, the most positive
response by far has been to a weekly fairtrade stall. This has
opened up many possibilities for conversation and has helped
to create for many people a sense that we are batting for the
same side.

## Working at the margins

Chaplaincy can feel both lonely and barren at times, for the
effect that chaplains have is often hidden, the results come
slowly, and the fruit might only be visible after many years.
In ministry, just as in most working lives, we are used to our
motivation coming from models of success. This is one reason
why the Church remains preoccupied by numbers. In higher
education chaplaincy there may be few regular activities by
which to judge success, and occasional events can often be
poorly attended and therefore feel unsuccessful. It is easy to
feel that the chaplaincy is indeed marginal. Much of our work
is about being engaged in a process rather than in particular
activities. It is about the need to bridge different worlds, making faith and spirituality both *intelligible* and *accessible*. This
can only be done by joining people where they are: by taking
part in conversations that show an interest in other people's
sphere of learning rather than in trying to make explicit references to faith or religion, by working in small groups, by

thinking outside the box, and by being ready for the unexpected. The focus must be on *presence* rather than *activity*. The greatest opportunity for chaplains to promote the Kingdom of God is by being alongside people in the learning environment, and to be seen to be sharing the values of higher education, values such as the importance of learning about learning, and the importance of developing the whole person. Only by showing a profound respect for these values can we hope that matters of faith may be given an equally respectful hearing. When through the work of the chaplaincy a student engages with questions of faith, at whatever level, there will be some occasions when this leads to a degree of involvement in chaplaincy activities, but there will be other times when it leads to someone exploring a local church some years down the line.

To establish a sense of presence in such a relatively large institution, partnership with others is essential. Being at the margins can be helpful, for at the margins denominational boundaries, and to a lesser extent divisions between the faiths, seem much less important. I can achieve very little on my own as a half-time Anglican. By sharing our resources, my Roman Catholic colleague (also half-time at Goldsmiths) and I can between us offer a regular weekly discussion group at the Catholic chaplaincy where there are facilities for providing a meal for the students who attend. There is little point in worrying which denomination people belong to.

## Working in separation

Although there are some signs that the Church of England is beginning to respond to the opportunities of higher education chaplaincy, including a debate in the February 2005 General Synod, by and large we are still viewed as peripheral by the dioceses in which we work. The college or university will also see most of us as outside the core aims of higher education. I am given no budget, either by the college or by the diocese (I am even expected to pay for my own Diocesan Directory).

Although I have an annual review within the college's Student Services Department, at the time of writing I am not within the programme of ministerial review in the diocese, although this is under consideration. As chaplains we need to take responsibility for our own support networks. It is tempting to use this as an excuse to quietly disengage from the rest of the Church, to use the freedom of our slightly detached situation to maintain a pattern and structure that suits our own situation and inclination, but that doesn't relate at all to the wider Church structures. So I can work in a loose team structure as the sole Anglican in an ecumenical and inter-faith team and relate on a very personal level with my colleagues, quietly ignoring those aspects of Anglicanism that I find problematic.

But if our experiences, our struggles and our insights are to inform the life and activity of the wider Church then we are going to have to engage with the wider Church at deanery and diocesan levels. Equally, the Church needs to ensure that the structures are open to receiving our insights.

## The joys of chaplaincy

What I have said about my experience so far at Goldsmiths has tended to focus on the difficulties of adjustment from parish ministry, and also on some of the tougher aspects of ministry in a secular environment. While it can be tough, at the same time it is good. There is an infectiously positive quality to the educational environment, and a refreshing willingness to explore questions and issues. In my experience of different careers, and different church environments, I can honestly say that overall the morale at Goldsmiths is higher than in any other place I have worked.

As I begin my third year here, some of the groundwork put in is beginning to bear fruit, and when positive feedback is received it is a great boost, such as a student telling me recently that the chaplaincy had made her glad to call herself Christian, after many years of disillusionment with the Church.

Although ministry is not comfortable in such a secular

context, the flip-side is that there are always new experiences of God's mission. The need for flexibility of response gives great freedom for constant innovation and for engagement with new ideas. The fact of belonging to a non-religious institution with large numbers of other people means that it is possible to cross many of the religious barriers that exist within our own structures. It would be unthinkable for me to undertake any piece of work here without considering the implications for ecumenical and inter-faith involvement. This not only helps to open up whole new dimensions of engagement and understanding, but it also creates a new sense of priorities: one that focuses less on the differences between people, and more on our common humanity.

And while the transient nature of the student population makes it difficult to have a sense of building up the Kingdom of God year on year, it does at least mean that every year is a new start.

## Further reading

Robinson, Simon, *Ministry Among Students: A Pastoral Theology and Handbook for Practice*, Canterbury Press, Norwich, 2004.

Church of England Board of Education, *Pillars of the Church: Supporting Chaplaincy in Further and Higher Education*, Church House Publishing, London, 2002.

Legood, Giles (ed.), *Chaplaincy: The Church's Sector Ministries*, Cassell, London, 1999.

Earwaker, John, *Helping and Supporting Students*, The Society for Research into Higher Education and Open University Press, Buckingham, 1992.

# 15. Serving in a Healing Community
## The Hospital Chaplain

### DAVID FLAGG

I was sick and you took care of me. (Matthew 25.36)

Fred is meeting me for the first time, and understandably blinks. He is sitting up in bed and I am giving him my usual patter: 'Good morning, I'm David, I'm one of the chaplains, just coming to say hello!' I see him searching for a response, and sense the thought pattern ('What do I say to a *chaplain*? . . . oh, I know, he's a *vicar*.') Fastening on what he thinks might be the right line, Fred responds, 'And where is your church?' It is an interesting reflection, not least because I am just arriving at the point where half of my ordained ministry has been spent in parish work and half as a healthcare chaplain.

## Differences

One difference that I notice a lot is that of journeys. As a parish priest, especially in a semi-rural setting, my day was punctuated by car journeys to and from various encounters. Such journeys provided space for both reflection and preparation. There was no journey 'to' work, because I worked from home. Now that I no longer live on the job, I have the rigours and delights (because of the clear boundaries it provides) of travelling to and from work. Once at work I ricochet around in a large but nevertheless confined space. Then again there is a more specific focus. In the variety of parish ministry I tended to accompany the same people through different life events. In hospital ministry, I tend to do much the same things each week, but with different people.

One crucial distinction is that healthcare chaplains, if like me they are full-time, have a secular employer. I am immersed in the immediate context of current National Health Service culture. So when I am introducing chaplaincy work to new staff in our hospital, I purposely use a definition of spirituality by writers on nursing:

> Spirituality is a quality that goes beyond religious affiliation, that strives for inspirations, reverence, awe, meaning and purpose, even in those who do not believe in any God. The spiritual dimension tries to be in harmony with the universe, strives for answers about the infinite, and comes into focus when the person faces emotional stress, physical illness or death.[1]

This differentiates spirituality from religion in a way that would not happen from within the bosom of the Church. Chaplains are asked to see themselves, not as the narrow providers of one religious product, though they may well specialize in one such, but as those who discern spiritual need of all kinds.

## Spiritual pain

A helpful way to describe what may happen in a chaplain's day is to see it as a response to 'spiritual pain', which may threaten to tear us apart deep inside. Typically, there are the questions about identity and meaning – such as 'Who am I?' – that surface in serious illness. A 25-year-old man diagnosed with an aggressive leukemia said: 'I feel like a totally different person.' The age-old questions we ask in adversity are 'Why?' and 'Why me?' This is not because we have read somewhere in the textbook of life that suffering requires us to ask 'Why?' Rather, it comes up from deep inside with its own originality. A prayer card left by a visitor reads: 'Why when we/I need our Christian God, is it only questions and no answers – why?[2] It may well be asked in anger, or in a real self-questioning. Patients sometimes start unpicking their lives to look for the reason why. That search transcends religious faiths. A Buddhist patient with whom I talked seemed to find some meaning in locating what she felt was the failure in her life as something that was now being worked out through her own 'karmic suffering'.

In hospital there is so much loss – loss of dignity, loss of privacy, loss of control. There is the crucial loss of secure surroundings. A cry we hear many times a day is simply 'I want to go home'. For those who have always been active there is the loss of those routine tasks that give life its meaning. An ordinand who visited our hospital for a day was struck that everyone was wearing pyjamas: a symbol of the 'stripping' admission to hospital requires. There can be a great deal of fear, because this is a journey into the unknown. Anger is quite possibly the most common emotion that a chaplain meets: anger tends to be our immediate response to enforced and unwelcome change. Sometimes the anger is blatant and sometimes it is suppressed or displaced, fastening as it can so easily do on to the many frustrations of hospital life. Two complaints feature in particular – the necessity of 'waiting' for everything; and the sense that 'nobody tells me anything'. However much NHS reforms move towards giving patients more sense of control and choice, it is unlikely that the pain of the felt helplessness will go away. I often reflect with patients on their very title : 'patient' implies an experience both of suffering (in its Latin root) and of waiting (in the meaning it has come to acquire).

## Listening

The chaplain in hospital, then, dares to enter into this sea of spiritual pain. What does he or she bring to this task? How is spiritual pain addressed or relieved? A key strategy is listening. By necessity clinical staff are focused on what they have to achieve for the patient in a practical sense. Chaplains and their teams, often of voluntary helpers with training and aptitude in the listening task, can be a prime resource in giving patients time and attention. What they find to listen to can never be predicted. It may be that the patient is in terrible physical pain and this is all they can focus on. But experience suggests that if a patient is given listening time, their repeated requests for pain relief in the form of medication may be lessened. It may be that they have just been talking to a doctor and they are assessing the impact of this conversation. It may be that they are reflecting very deeply on their lives and that the chaplain's visit coincides with this. The consequent discussion may be not unlike a spiritual direction session. But we never know exactly what will happen when we set out. I always say to students on placement that there is nothing we can *make* happen when we visit and there is nothing we can *stop* happening. We may start out, as I did with a student on her first visit, to give someone holy communion and end up (literally) holding the vomit bowl.

Active listening – the attentive offering of oneself – is a gift in itself. It often takes time (though strangely a highly empathetic encounter can sometimes be quite brief) and it always takes energy. It is not restricted to words. One of the challenges is listening to those who may not be able to speak. The temptation is to try and say something, as if we had better talk since they cannot. But doing without words can bring us to things more basic and essentially more human, like sight and touch. I shall always remember the agony communicated through the eyes of a woman in her fifties who had suffered a stroke. She could not speak, yet her gaze spoke volumes. We had several quite brief encounters in which eye contact and, crucially, holding her by the hand, were the main components.

When she left to go home, she thanked me for my help. I said, as we all do, that I had not done anything, and she replied quite emphatically, 'Oh yes you did'.

## Results

What can happen for patients as this gift of loving attention is offered can also never be predicted. A young man recovering from an unpleasant operation put it : 'You kept me sane.' Listening time is equally appreciated by the families and friends surrounding a seriously ill patient, and this is maybe where a chaplain gives their main input. It can seem like simple chatting after saying 'hello' on the corridor where people sit outside Intensive Care. Work done in corridors is often unknown and cannot easily be quantified. The widow of a patient who died asked if one of the chaplains could take his funeral. But she did not ask for the chaplain who had occasionally visited him and chatted; rather she wanted 'that nice lady who smiles at me in the corridor'. It may be the provision of quiet and reflective space, which is valued. The family of a seriously ill patient can be helped by regular visits to a prayer room where they can leave messages on a prayer board, and take time to sit or weep, with or without a member of the chaplaincy team.

Spiritual care then can consist of quite simple actions, which somehow further 'what love requires'. I remember the man whose eyes met mine on the ward. He told me how sometimes, especially at night, everything looked very dark. He was frustrated by the ongoing effects of rheumatoid arthritis. So I took him a little prayer card with nothing but a candle on it: something to 'lighten' the darkness. A day or two later he remarked, 'I've accepted it now'. Adjusting to limitations and to losses can be helped by such an easing of the path. Buddhist meditation for example is largely about learning to live with impermanence. Discovering some spiritual stability enables us to face the necessary 'changes and chances of this fleeting world', as the prayer in the order for Night Prayer puts it. There can even be growth in the midst of diminishments. I heard this expressed very authentically by a middle-aged man with HIV, who said simply, 'As I get smaller and weaker He gets bigger and stronger'. This man particularly valued attending a simple Eucharist.

Religious habits may well help, like receiving holy communion and anointing with oil. Chaplains pick up some of their referrals from priests and pastors commending church members to their care. Going on receiving communion for example means that you are not completely dislocated from your spiritual fellowship. However, some churchgoers initially baulk at the minister coming to them: up to now this has been about them 'going to church for that'. Others instinctively return to the sacraments or discover them for the first time. A local vicar was stopped, when visiting a ward, by a lady who said she wanted to be confirmed. The vicar referred her to me, and when I spoke to her it became clear that her not being confirmed had been an oversight when she was a teenager. Without prompting, she recited the Apostles' Creed to me faultlessly, and I asked her if she would like communion; I said we could discuss possible confirmation at another point. She was a little breathless, and after receiving communion she sank back on her pillows with the words 'Now I belong!' Two days later I went to look for her again, only to be told that she had died shortly after that communion visit. This encounter reveals that much of our work is done by being *seen* as much as by getting formal referrals. It also demonstrates the value of collaboration between local clergy visiting in a hospital and the chaplaincy team, and it gives a feel of the way chaplaincy operates on the edge of church structures and demonstrates a different way of being church where people are at the extremities of their experience. 'And where is your church?' resonates here. Chaplains can be flexible about church regulations, where these may impede good spiritual care. Communion for example is normally offered to all those who feel they would benefit from it. A later regularizing of this can be pursued on discharge through referral to local parishes.

Faith is always unique to each of us. A woman in her early fifties whom I met on the oncology unit told me that she had found her faith in her illness in a way that could not have been achieved without being ill. Like many people who are bed-bound but lucky enough to be near a window, she spent a lot of time looking at the sky. One day, in the middle of the clouds, she clearly 'saw' the face of Jesus. Simply writing this down fails to capture what that moment meant for her. In the depths of spiritual pain, and at the edges of our physical exist-ence (she went home and died within weeks) such moments happen. I learned that the dawning of a new faith can happen in a hospital bed with nothing to see but the sky.

The question can (and should) be asked as to the precise role of the chaplain in such an experience. As we reflect on such moments, we may well come back to the simple idea of accompaniment. In spiritual care we travel with people on their spiritual journey, and as companions we witness and affirm what happens along the way. So often patients say: 'I haven't told anyone this because it sounds quite mad, but I feel I can tell you.' Accompaniment in the musical sense is also active: the accompanist joins in but does not overwhelm. We have a part to play.

## Healing, dying and bereavement

There can be an unnecessary suspicion between hospital chaplaincy and the Church's healing ministry. This may be about the latter's perceived disregard of medical prognosis in favour of the interventions of a higher power, compared to the healthcare chaplain's commitment to good practice and their understanding of the danger that vulnerable people can be manipulated by religious people's prayers. Yet all of us know situations where patients have been prayed over *in extremis* (and maybe the prayers have been for a good death) who have subsequently made a good recovery.

However much they might not wish to be seen in this light, hospital chaplains are often viewed, sometimes humorously and sometimes with real fright, as angels of death. The vast majority of emergency calls out of hours in acute hospitals are about a patient who is imminently dying or about a family asking for prayers after a patient has died. Chaplains often collaborate with palliative care teams to generate the kind of quality of care for the dying afforded to those in hospices. Occasionally we witness what might be described as a 'good death'. But normally dying is a struggle punctuated, if we are fortunate, by moments of inspiration and hope. There will also be cultural difference. When a Zimbabwean man lay dying his wife declined further help from me after I had clearly agreed with the doctors' view that he was dying. I was merely attempting to support her and her young sons in what I supposed was their necessary process of grief. When I consulted a Zimbabwean friend he put me straight: 'You see, for them, if you talk about it you will make it happen.' The current Western desire to try and facilitate what we think of as a good death and healthy grief has to be modified in the light of how a family within their own cultural setting may operate, and what they can bear at any one point.

Similarly, in the area of pregnancy loss, where chaplains often become involved, it is possible that a West African woman may *not* want to look at her dead baby or attend the funeral. In her traditional culture (often dependent on local geography) shame attaches to this, and mothers never attend the funerals of their own children. Her received wisdom is to look forward, not back. Western approaches to grieving may want to challenge this, but some recent research has suggested that the mental well-being of mothers is not necessarily promoted by pressure to clothe and hold their dead babies. It is important for us to affirm whatever helps the bereaved at the point where they are. But this can be a perilously difficult path when people are caught between cultures, and when we ourselves inevitably convey a sense of our own beliefs.

Bereavement is a key area for chaplains to be involved in. Few NHS Trusts provide any other psychological or emotional support for the bereaved. Sudden and tragic bereavement often occurs, especially in Accident and Emergency departments. I met a woman early one morning who could not be prized away from the body of her husband who had died suddenly in middle age. She could not bear for me to pray because that would imply that she was saying goodbye. In such situations the chaplain feels – there is no other word – helpless. There is a temptation to run away: 'There is nothing I can do, so why stay?' This question needs asking with discernment, because on occasions it is right, perhaps having met a required religious need, to withdraw. But not always. At such times we see very clearly that spiritual care is not finally about *doing* something; it is much more about *being*, and at that moment it is about being *there*, where the awfulness is happening. Six months later she wrote me a card: 'Since that moment of terrible loss I've been driven almost insane by grief. You came to me, to light the beacon in the darkness, again and again. Would you always be available for people like me?' I referred her on to weekly bereavement counselling, which benefited her, but she also wanted an ongoing connection with me. When we are there sharing a moment of terrible loss, then *we ourselves* can become associated with the dead person in the bereaved person's mind. Providing regular remembrance services is one way in which chaplaincies can maintain such relationships and encourage grief to be shared.

## Skills and survival

These illustrations from a chaplain's diary show that he or she needs a wide armoury of capabilities, including a familiarity with NHS culture, awareness of pastoral counselling approaches, good communication skills, and the ability to steer a strategic course at the same time as being interruptable. In pastoral care, which is its own art-form, we learn the knack of using ourselves for the benefit of others. Self-awareness is essential. So like all ministers who give time to others, we need to pay attention to our own needs for survival and nurture, not least of our own spiritual life. We will, consciously or unconsciously, seek survival mechanisms. For example, most chaplains don't spend ten hours a day actually going round wards meeting patients. When a study of hospital chaplains in the London area was published, the headline in the *Church Times* read 'Chaplains avoid patients'.[2] Administrative chores, time to reflect, attendance at management meetings, professional gatherings such as a clinical ethics committee, and teaching, are essential complements to the demands of patient contact. Hopefully there can be a balance in the kind of pastoral encounters we undertake, so a very intense situation might be followed by a more social conversation. One of the pressures is that of providing emergency cover outside normal working hours. Even if the number of calls is few, there is nevertheless a mental and social stress in having to hold yourself ready. But, where there are colleagues to share the load, the boundaries of availability are clearer than in parish ministry.

Two lifelines are essential. First, 'recognized professional supervision for their practice in clinical settings' is a requirement in the professional standards set out by the College of Health Care Chaplains. This should normally be undertaken off-site on a regular basis, in my view at least monthly, with someone outside your situation. It has all kinds of benefits, from releasing some of the emotional build-up, to discovering blindspots and developing new strategies. The second lifeline lies in the spiritual nurture provided by your own faith community. This is one way of answering that question 'And where is your church?' – I sometimes say that I go to church where I live and do not have to worry about looking after it! A faith-base of your own, a spiritual director or confessor, retreats, theological reflection with others – such resources are vital.

## A bridging place

Healthcare chaplaincy, maybe more than any other sector ministry, acts as a kind of bridging place between the faith community and the professional work setting. So a chaplain is employed by the NHS, but must also be authorized by his or her own faith community. An Anglican priest must therefore hold the licence of the bishop in whose diocese they work. As the trends continue towards professionalizing healthcare chaplaincy, rootedness in a faith community is going to be more and more important. Without this we are in danger of producing a kind of hybrid species called 'healthcare chaplains'. The bishop of St Albans, when licensing a chaplain in 1997, spoke of the need for chaplains to have a 'defiant language system' to challenge the thoughts and assumptions of NHS culture.

That culture is currently eating into the ways in which hospital chaplains used to see themselves. A key difference is that of confidentiality. When I was a curate 25 years ago, my incumbent (who was 20 years older than me) would arrive at the hospital reception desk and survey the admission register, which simply sat there. He would note down all the names and addresses of recently admitted patients who resided in his parish and proceed to call on them. That situation would be unthinkable now. As a result of the Data Protection Act 1998 and of guidelines on confidentiality, chaplains are no longer party to any information about patients unless it is with the specific permission of those patients. This has led to the crazy situation where in some hospitals patients may be asked if they have a faith or religion, but this information cannot be passed on to the chaplaincy service. I never followed my incumbent's model, and in general I prefer today's arrangements, which are more respectful of a patient's expressed wishes. There are many other changes. What is sometimes called a service-delivery model in which 'evidence-based practice' can be monitored and evaluated, is currently being pressed on to chaplaincy. But evaluation of this kind cannot actually describe what spiritual ministry brings to a patient or to the hospital at large. This is why remaining an integral part of our own spiritual tradition is vital, in order to keep alive an awareness of the very real mysteries that no management tool can fathom.

## Hospital as community

The new trends are not happening without debate. Voices
have been raised in favour of the kind of chaplain who is a
friend to all and whose strength lies in remaining outside the
organizational structures so that they can slide in at any level
to 'have a word'. In reality, of course, however developed the
management frameworks might become, the way to make
things happen is still through positive interpersonal engagement. Wise managers still instinctively seek out chaplains and
welcome their insights, because they are known to have their
'ear to the ground'. Whatever the current language of management, a hospital is a community, with its own distinctive
life and, one might say, spirituality. I work in a 'new build'
hospital where modern facilities do not of themselves create
an atmosphere of care and healing. Down the road from us
was the famous Brook Hospital, now demolished. Many of
our staff used to work there, and they tell me that in spite of
its bedraggled condition they would far rather go back there
because of what they describe as its family atmosphere. Recognition of the need for this often hidden 'X factor' may yet
become the focus of organizational strategies. Chaplains help
to remind the organization that it forgets its identity as a community at its peril.

Included in the community of the hospital are its staff,
and chaplains not only work alongside them but also offer
them a listening ear. In our hospital the prayer room is well
used each day by members of staff. The chaplaincy team co-
ordinate a Contact Officer scheme for staff who are harassed
or under pressure. We also debrief distressing situations with
the maternity staff team. Chaplains may well be called upon
for their teaching abilities, especially in areas like bereavement and the care of the dying, and to help medical staff with
the skills required to impart difficult information.

## A diverse community

Whoever leads the spiritual care service will have 'meeting the spiritual and religious needs of all' as one of their key responsibilities. They will be managing leaders from all faiths, either as volunteer members of their team or increasingly as paid (though still mainly part-time) chaplains. Such a manager does not need to be a Christian minister, nor an Anglican one. Multi-faith diversity is not simply paying lip-service to a politically correct agenda. Because a hospital serves a wide community, it is likely to embrace a number of diverse groupings. This is true of the Borough of Greenwich in which I work, which has one of the widest cross-sections, ethnically, socio-economically and religiously. When we recently added a Sikh volunteer member to our chaplaincy team we found that she had a network of contacts born of the closeness of the Punjabi community, quite different to but just as impressive as the Anglican parish networks with which we were already working. Because we have a recently built hospital we have one shared prayer room for all to use. Older hospitals are having to adapt their Christian chapels, or, as is more common, to provide an additional multi-faith prayer space. Having just one space, as we do, adds further interest to that question, 'And where is your church?' The place where I pray and gather with others to celebrate Christian liturgy is also the place where Muslims come several times a day to pray, and where they too gather together. Such rich experience may yet demonstrate new ways of being church and of sharing sacred spaces. When I come into our simple prayer room, I often see two people praying side by side who have quite different religious beliefs and traditions. All those who regularly pray in this shared space have some sense of being soul friends. It says something very powerful to the world in which we live, in which a threatened clash of civilizations is neither the final nor the true word.

## Christ in the pain

Someone has just written three words on our prayer board:
'Love is All'.

Are 'hospitals' about 'hospitality'? One of the tasks chaplaincy can attempt is to model loving hospitality by keeping
alive the human and the personal within what can be experienced as a cruelly impersonal system. In St Benedict's Rule,
every guest was to be received as if they were Christ himself, who was to be adored in them. That old-world wisdom
coincides with one of the recent government initiatives from
the 1997 NHS Plan – 'Improving The Patient Experience'.
Focusing on the patient could mean that chaplains let go of
needing to 'take Christ' or 'be Christ', as if the strong ever
mediate God to the weak. We may begin to see Christ himself
in the patient, revealed there as suffering love transfiguring
the very darkness of spiritual pain.

So one answer to 'And where is your church?' is immediate:
'It is here and it is now'.

### Further reading

Orchard, Helen (ed.), *Spirituality in Health Care Contexts*, Jessica
　　Kingsley, London, 2001.
Speck, Peter, *Being There: Care in Time of Illness*, New Library of
　　Pastoral Care, SPCK, London, 1988.
Wilson, Simon, *When I Was in Hospital You Visited Me*, Grove Pastoral
　　Series 88, Grove Books, Cambridge, 2001.

### Notes

1 Murray, R. B. and Zentner, J. B., *Nursing Concepts for Health
Promotion*, Prentice-Hall, New York, 1989.
2 Orchard, Helen (ed.), *Hospital Chaplaincy – Modern, Depend-
able?* Sheffield Academic Press, Sheffield, 2000.

# 16. While We're Here, We Belong
## The Stipendiary Incumbent

### MALCOLM TORRY

I do not want to see you now just in passing, for I hope to spend some time with you, if the Lord permits (1 Corinthians 16.7)

'Is the vicar in?' No, but he or she soon will be. 'Are you the vicar?' The answer's likely to be 'Yes', because this is the vicarage: either it's next door to the church, or its address is on the church noticeboard. 'Come in' – because the vicar's got time. She's just conducted a school assembly and has an hour to spare before a funeral. 'This is St John's Vicarage. If you would like to leave a message, please speak slowly and clearly after the tone, not forgetting to leave your name and number' – because people do forget. They expect you to be there, every minute of every day, and don't expect to have to speak to an answering machine. They expect you to be there, because that's what you're for; and they expect you to be out in the parish, caring for its people, because that's what you're for as well.

This chapter is about the stipendiary *incumbent*:[1] the paid priest licensed to serve a parish or parishes. And this chapter is about the *stipendiary* incumbent, and so will differ in many respects from the chapters about the *non*-stipendiary priest and the Ordained Local Minister – though all three chapters are, of course, about being a *priest*.

The priest's task is laid out in the Ordinal, in the bishop's words to those who are about to be ordained:

> A priest is called by God to work with the bishop and with his fellow-priests, as servant and shepherd among the people to whom he is sent. He is to proclaim the word of the Lord, to call his hearers to repentance, and in Christ's name to absolve and to declare the forgiveness of sins. He is to baptize and prepare the baptized for Confirmation. He is to preside at the celebration of the Holy Communion. He is to lead his people in prayer and worship, to intercede for them, to bless them in the name of the Lord, and to teach and encourage by word and example. He is to minister to the sick, and prepare the dying for their death. He must set the Good Shepherd always before him as the pattern of his calling, caring for the people committed to his charge, and joining with them in a common witness to the world.[2]

These tasks and roles are common to all priests, whether stipendiary or not and whether an incumbent or not.

## The incumbent

Above all, the incumbent *belongs* – so they are a member of the community and a member of the congregation, and at the same time they have a leadership role in the congregation and a representative role in the community.

### The incumbent in the congregation

Whether the clergy are members of the 'laity', 'the people', is an interesting issue. Theoretically, in the Roman Catholic Church, priests are now members of the People of God and not separated from it; and in the Church of England too baptism is *the* fundamental initiation, and ordination is of a secondary status. But that's not always how it feels. At every level in the Church's governing structures, clergy and laity (that is, non-clergy laity) are divided into separate 'houses', which often vote separately; and on Maundy Thursday, when we reaffirm our ordination vows in the cathedral, some clergy speak as the 'people' promise to support the clergy, and some don't.

But when it comes to the congregation as a group of people gathering for worship in a particular place, the incumbent *belongs*. We might paste up the posters, carry the furniture, bring a dish to bring and share lunches, deliver the Christmas cards along with everyone else, and we join the choir when there aren't enough tenors.

*And* the incumbent has a *leadership* role. We preside at worship (and invite or give permission to others to preside and preach). We chair Parochial Church Council meetings (though some of us preside over a rotating of the chair, because all of us are members – more on chairing below). There are certain decisions that are ours to take (though not many, whatever the common perception might be – including the common perception of many clergy).

It is this combination of belonging and leading that gives the role of the incumbent its interest and its uniqueness. In one respect every member of a congregation belongs in precisely the same way: we are all of us baptized, we are all of us present for worship, and we all stack the chairs. In another respect the incumbent's position is *un*like anyone else's: he or she is the only one who *has* to be there, is the one who presides (or gives permission to someone else to do so), and is the one who decides on the details of the liturgy in consultation with others – yes, always in consultation, but it is still the incumbent's decision. Because the incumbent is a member like other members, he or she might *not* be involved in parts of the congregation's life: they might *not* be in the banner-making group, might *not* teach the children's church (though they might); might *not* attend the building committee (though they could if they wished). But if the incumbent is a wise leader then they will remain in touch, will affirm the creativity, will create communication, will value people's gifts, and will encourage people to discover and to use their talents.

The leadership role is diverse and difficult to define, and the particular leadership tasks don't really get to the heart of it – for the heart of it is not located at any kind of 'centre' of the life of the congregation but is rather on the boundary between the local and the universal. When the bishop gives a priest a licence, he tells the priest that the cure of souls is both his and theirs. The bishop is one bishop among many, and potentially – if ever the Church's structures come to reflect the unity for which Jesus prayed – the bishop is the representative of the Church universal in his diocese and the priest shares in that representation. It is through his or her ordination that the priest comes to be a representative figure, and in their parish they *are* the representative of the Church universal in a way in which no one else can be – which is why they attend clergy chapter meetings, Deanery Synod meetings and diocesan conferences and events, in order to fulfil their responsibility to enact the link between their congregation or congregations and the wider Church.

But the incumbent is not simply a representative of the bishop as they have both the right and the ability to lead the congregation in opposition to the bishop. Neither in theory nor in practice is the congregation a local branch of a national organization: it is in itself both a complete expression of the universal Church and an organization (and indeed a charity) in its own right. It is therefore possible for a congregation's members to regard their congregation as *the* Church and to resent the sending of resources elsewhere, even if those resources go in an equitable fashion to support the work of the diocese's parishes as a whole.

The incumbent can thus find him- or herself in a most interesting position: as both the bishop's representative (and as representing decisions of the General and Diocesan Synods to the parish), and as incumbent of a particular parish and a member of that congregation, and in some cases standing against the bishop in defence of the parish and of its views and practices and maybe of its existence. (The situation also means, of course, that the incumbent can find him- or herself both against the congregation *and* against the bishop: at which point it's probably time to think of a career change.)

The bishop will visit his parishes, and we welcome him when he comes. We fill his day, with morning prayer, a visit to a school, taking communion to someone housebound, a visit to the sheltered accommodation, a visit to some industry in the parish, a meeting with the churchwardens, Evening Prayer, a meeting of the Parochial Church Council – and there might be time to eat. But we can refuse a bishop's visit, and it happens. This is all as it should be. The parish is the heart of the Church of England, and every parish is different, each in its own place with its own diverse population, its own building, and its own congregation – which will be unlike any other congregation. Any attempt at centralized management of a diocese's parishes would be a disaster. The Church of England's system of government, with authority scattered everywhere imaginable, and with the Parochial Church Council and the incumbent each with their own powers and each tied inexorably to the other, is absolutely right, for it gives to the parish the autonomy necessary to adapt to its context and to adapt to new circumstances – and in South London in particular, in this particular century, new circumstances are coming at us thick and fast. The Church of England's system of government is up to the task.

In the congregation the incumbent is both member and leader – and central to these roles is the church building.

## The incumbent in the church building

An important part of the incumbent's freehold is their freehold of the church building. With the churchwardens the incumbent is responsible for the building and, in a way unique in English law, the building *belongs* to the incumbent. This doesn't mean that they can sell it, or that they can do what they like with it, but it does mean that it is their responsibility. The incumbent's task is to pray in it, to look after it, to make it available for worship (and ensure that worship is its primary task), to welcome people into it, and to use it for mission.

So when a school class comes, because religious buildings are on the curriculum, the incumbent welcomes them and introduces them to the activities that go on in the building. And when disasters occur, or local celebrations need some space, or a public meeting is too big for the hall next door, then the incumbent makes the building available.

But never alone: for the churchwardens are the people's representatives, and significantly are elected by anyone who lives in the parish who turns up to vote (again, this is as it should be, for the building is held in trust for the parish as a whole, and not only for the congregation that meets in it). Once a year it is the churchwardens who welcome the arch-deacon or the rural dean for an annual inspection; and always it is the churchwardens and the incumbent together who manage the building and are answerable for its use, for its repair, and for any changes made to it – so it is they who sign applications for permission to make those changes.

Primary school children, having met me in the church build-ing, are sometimes surprised to find that I don't live there. Their presupposition is not inappropriate. While the church building is in no sense the whole of an incumbent's ministry, it is an important part of it, and there is a proper bond of affection and of belonging to the building. This is why serious problems with the building can blight the whole of an incum-bent's ministry, and why the building's destruction can be deeply traumatic, for it affects the community and the con-gregation. Thus in three ways it affects the incumbent, who is so closely identified with the building, who is a member of the congregation as well as its leader, and who represents the Church to the community and makes the building available to the community.

## The incumbent in the community

The parish is a place (it has boundaries), and the incumbent's responsibility is to the place and to all of its people, including those who belong to some other religious organization. If they need something from the Church – some spiritual sustenance, a place to pray, someone to talk to, a relative's funeral conducted, a marriage, a baptism (and when I was an incumbent in New Cross it was a pleasure to baptize the children of members of a local black-led Pentecostal church) – whatever it is (well, almost whatever), it's our responsibility to make sure it happens. The parish structure of the Church of England is a theological statement, and is itself a kind of sacrament, for it expresses the grace of God, a love without condition, a love for all, whatever their allegiances – and at the same time it ensures that that kind of love happens. So if ever the Church of England *were* to be disestablished, and for ecumenical and other reasons it might be right that it should be, then care *must* be taken to ensure that the parish system isn't abolished along with its establishment. The relationship of the congregation, the building and the incumbent to *every* person in the community is a theological statement that, once lost, could never be recreated.

The incumbent is still sometimes called the 'parson', that is, a 'person' who is there for the community at large – and sometimes for the community over against the wider Church and sometimes over against the congregation. What should an incumbent do if churchgoing is a condition for admission to a church school? Some parents will be able to attend church regularly in order to get their children to a desirable school, but some parents either can't or won't. And some of the children thus excluded might be more in need of the education the school offers than some of the children who get in. Does the incumbent, who will usually be a governor, and sometimes the chair of governors, try to change the criteria? Or do they defend the churchgoing criterion (because it brings people into church)? Or do they keep their head down? These are real questions, and the answers tell us where the incumbent sees the focus of their ministry: in the parish's community, in the congregation, or both.

Just as the incumbent belongs to the congregation, so the incumbent belongs to the community. So it is as important to contribute to local arts festivals, to defend the local library, and to attend meetings about the future of a housing estate, as it is to say Morning Prayer and to prepare new Christians for baptism and confirmation. Many tasks, of course, belong to both congregation and community: a funeral in church might be a congregational event and a community event; the school crossing lady being confirmed might be a community event as well as a congregational event; and an arts festival, partly held in the church building, might encourage people to come to the festival service on the Sunday morning as well as being a secular community event. And this is as it should be, for the congregation belongs to the community – at least, it should do. In some parishes, where the congregation comes from a large hinterland because they like the style of religion on offer, the incumbent might find some disjunction between their role in the community and their role in the congregation. A congregation can remain firmly related to its community even if many of its members come from elsewhere, provided it sees that relationship as essential to its mission (and not just for the sake of evangelism); but where very few in the congregation regard the parish's community as their responsibility, and where the incumbent's focus is in the congregation and maybe in some particular brand of religion and its networks and institutions, then the parish will not be what it should be: a place, a community, a congregation, a building, and a pastor, all intimately involved with each other. The Church of England's specific task is closely bound up with the nature of the parish, and the incumbent in particular will have a diminished and less fulfilling role if the links are broken.

There are a number of consequences of the incumbent's relationship with both the community and the congregation.

If the incumbent is married, the question arises, both in the congregation and in the community, as to what extent the partner is their own person and to what extent they are the spouse of the incumbent. They are, of course, both, but that doesn't answer the question as to how they are viewed by people in the parish. The stereotypical 'vicar's wife', while she still exists, is now rare: and the existence of an increasing number of spouses of female clergy is hastening the role's demise. But clarity is still needed. People sometimes expect my wife Rebecca to know things they've told me because I'm the parish priest, and she doesn't, and they are surprised. There is still a lingering expectation that Rebecca is somehow an extension of my role, which is not how she sees herself. She has her own career, and is a member of the congregation and of the community in the way in which she would be if I was not the parish's incumbent.

Second, if the incumbent has school-age children, a particularly fraught issue is where will they go to school? In some places this isn't an issue as there is only one state school and no private schools nearby. In South London it *is* an issue. There are lots of state schools within travelling distance, often of differing types, offering different educational experiences and different admissions criteria; and there are private schools, often offering scholarships for the children of clergy. The incumbent might identify with part of their community if their children go to private schools, and with another part if they go to state schools – and with part of the congregation if they go to private schools, and with another part if they go to state schools. And if their children go to selective state schools (whether selection is by the virtues listed in the primary school's report, by churchgoing, or by being good at football) then the questions get even more complicated. Given that every parent wants the best for their children, and will often and understandably compromise other principles to achieve that, then the incumbent can be faced with a question with no obviously right answer and thus only a series of wrong ones.

What *is* important is that the issues should be *discussed*, for the incumbent and his or her family are members of the

community, their family might be members of the congregation, and they certainly are. Belonging implies communication. In the end it matters more that the incumbent is part of
a whole community's debate over schooling than that they
make a particular decision over the education of their own
children. (In case any readers wish to know, our children
went to Haberdashers' Aske's, a local authority comprehensive school with foundation governors, which became a City
Technology College and then an Academy – which only goes
to show how complex the issue can become.)

There are both opportunities and potential problems for
the children of stipendiary clergy. Their childhood will often
be full of stimulating activities and of a multitude of different kinds of relationship with the people they get to know in
the community and in the congregation simply because those
people pass through their home. The potential problem is a
lack of the privacy that families and their children need, at
least for some of the time. Protecting days off, and being able
to go away together, are essential.

In relation to both spouse and children, decisions made
within the family might have an impact on the incumbent's
ministry, and the relationship between the incumbent and
the community and the congregation will have an impact on
the family. Complete clarity about roles is impossible, but it's
important to obtain as much as possible.

A third important consequence of the bond between
the incumbent and the community is that the choice of the
incumbent must have as much to do with the nature of the
community as it has to do with the nature of the congregation.
It was absolutely right that when I was incumbent of St
Catherine's, Hatcham, at New Cross, Owen Beament was
incumbent of All Saints, the next parish. He is passionate
about football and about Millwall Football Club, which was
in his parish. He is its chaplain. I could never have been. And
it is an equal pleasure that the Rector of Charlton is Jeffrey
Heskins, who is equally passionate about football and is
Charlton Athletic's chaplain. It is surely an act of Providence,

as well as of patrons and churchwardens, that I am in a parish
with no football club and Jeff is incumbent of a parish with a
club in the premiership.

A fourth consequence is that incumbents must take care
*how* they belong to local organizations. As a member of the
community, I belong to the Westcombe Society, a local group
that runs an excellent community newspaper and organizes
events such as a Christmas Fair, a Summer Fun Day, and
teas for elderly people. I am not on its management committee. There are events over which the Society and St George's
Church collaborate, and it is important that I can represent
the Church in the necessary discussions. If I were to be a
member of the Society's management committee then such
inter-organizational communication would become rather
complex. Where a parish's clergy and congregation are having difficulty relating to another local organization, it might
be that the distance between them is too great – or it might be
that it isn't great enough.

The incumbent's role will often be complex. When he or
she visits the local comprehensive school with their child who
is approaching secondary transfer, do they visit as parent or
as incumbent? As both, of course, for there is (or there should
be) an existing relationship between the incumbent and the
school. And if the child then goes to another school because
they've been sent privately, or they've passed the eleven plus
in the next borough, or they preferred another state comprehensive not in the parish, then has the incumbent made that
decision as a parent or as the parish's incumbent? Again, as
both – and the incumbent will experience the consequences.

In relation to the community as a whole, the situation is
inevitably complex, for the same person might be incumbent,
parent, resident, local activist, school governor, and maybe
even local councillor. If possible, the incumbent and the parish
must be clear that there are various *different* roles here, that
they are not the same, and that the boundaries between them
must be understood and protected, at least to some extent.

The other boundaries to which the incumbent might need

to give attention are those of the parish itself. If the natural community and the parish coincide, then the congregation, the community and the incumbent will all find life easier. It really didn't help when the Blackwall Tunnel approach road was built through the Parish of East Greenwich; and, more recently, when the Rochester Way relief road was built through the Parish of Kidbrooke. Suddenly new community boundaries were created, and it wasn't always obvious what should be done about parish boundaries.

Another of the boundaries that an incumbent needs to negotiate are those between different denominations. The Roman Catholic Church has a parish system, but with less sense that caring for the whole community is the Church's responsibility. The Free Churches have no parish boundaries, and, while a congregation will take responsibility in their community, it will be on an ad hoc basis. If the whole world is one's parish then actually nowhere is. Because the Church of England parish is a place of *responsibility*, it will often be the Church of England incumbent who initiates relationships between the Church and secular society and its institutions. Thus it was natural for me to phone up the developer of the Greenwich Peninsula as soon as they were appointed. The chaplaincy to the development quickly became a multi-faith project, but it is significant that the initiative was from within a Church of England parish. Yes, a kind of imperialism can be a danger here, particularly as the Church of England has greater resources and better territorial coverage than the other denominations (both of these factors being themselves consequences of the parish system, of course). But that danger should not stop us fulfilling an initiating role. If an organization is looking for a relationship with the Church in a particular place, then they'll know that that place has an incumbent, and they'll phone them up.

This gives us *two* responsibilities: one is to be willing to initiate where that is appropriate; the other is to ensure that as soon as possible the activity becomes ecumenical, and then maybe multi-faith, and that in those relationships the Church of England becomes an equal partner with other churches and faith groups.

All of this initiative and involvement, all of these relationships, happen because the incumbent has *time* – because he or she is *stipendiary*.

## The stipendiary incumbent

It is, to put it mildly, a privilege to be paid sufficient and to be provided with a house to enable me to serve the gospel, the Church, and the parish: its community and its congregation. I am paid a stipend: that is, enough to live on. It isn't a salary, as all clergy receive the same. There is no job description, there are no increments: there is simply the privilege of being given time to live a life that expresses my deepest convictions.

Unlike the Non-stipendiary priest or Ordained Local Minister in a full-time job, the stipendiary priest has *time*, a diary over which they have control (so don't believe a stipendiary priest who can't see you until three weeks' time), and large amounts of time when necessary. Having time available makes going to events possible, it means that the incumbent will often be at the heart of relationship networks in a community or in a borough, and it means that the incumbent will know people and will know who to talk to if something needs doing. These are the roots of the incumbent's effective relationship with their community, a major means of mission for the Church, and a major connection between the congregation and its community. Having time available means that the incumbent can do the jobs no one else is able or willing to do, whether the administration, painting a wall, doing the photocopying, or cutting the grass. Having time available means that the incumbent *can* spend time in prayer and in study of the Scriptures: both a privilege and a responsibility.

When in Mottingham a new 'learning shop' opened on the estate, a resource for the whole community, it was no surprise that Margaret Jackson, the incumbent, was intimately involved; and when in Bellingham racism needs tackling,

along with a variety of other community issues, wherever
you look Paul Butler, the vicar, is involved – because for these
incumbents, and for many others, prayer and social justice
simply can't be separated. And in both of these cases members
of the congregations are involved too – for the incumbent's
involvement will normally follow from other congregational
members' involvement, or will lead to it. In south London,
and elsewhere, wherever regeneration of communities is
occurring, the vicar will often be there – indeed, often before
the regeneration is even talked about – because the incumbent
is both incumbent and stipendiary: a representative figure,
involved in networks, and with the time to spend on them.

And it is because there is time that incumbents' diaries will
often contain such a variety of activity. Yes, there are incumbents who say Morning and Evening Prayer, lead worship on
Sundays, baptize, marry, conduct funerals, visit the sick, and
that's it – but they are rare, and they are missing out on the
opportunity for responsibility and for the stimulation variety can offer. Before the Greenwich District Hospital closed,
my former colleague, Christopher Morgan, was a part-time
chaplain there – a demanding and absorbing ministry. I am an
industrial chaplain in the parish (see Chapter 12). And there
are further and higher education chaplaincies, secondary
school chaplaincies, and many other opportunities for diverse
pastoral activity.

Because we are largely in control of our own diaries,
incumbents will often undertake responsibilities for the
wider Church. It has been a pleasure to be an Area Director
of Ordinands, helping to select candidates for ordination; to
be a rural dean (see the glossary); to teach Christian doctrine
on ordination and certificate courses; to convene a diocesan
theological study group; and to be on the council of a mission
society. Other clergy give time to developing and promoting
particular parties in the Church. They do this on behalf of us
all, because however much we might disagree with a particular group, one of the joys of the Church of England, and one
of the things that enables it to adapt to new circumstances and

to proclaim the gospel within them, is people's ability to think freely and to debate vigorously the most important issues facing us. For the same reason it is important that clergy continue to study and to do research, and our control over our diaries enables us to do that.

And some of us are rather old-fashioned. From the Reformation onwards, and to some extent before then, incumbents have been actively involved among the secular disciplines: economics, natural history, physics, literature . . . My own interests are in the nature and management of religious organizations (an example of a discipline both religious and secular), the reform of social security systems, and the philosophy of religion. Various of my neighbours have significant interests in the social sciences, the history of Western art, and paranormal phenomena. Further afield, contemporary philosophy seems to be quite a favourite in the Diocese of Southwark. We might not wish to emulate the personality and relationships of Mr Casaubon, the incumbent in George Eliot's *Middlemarch*, but his fascination with the history of mythology is something from which we could all learn. For by pursuing secular disciplines we serve both the Church and the world, building bridges across which the gospel can be expressed and across which the Church can learn more about the context in which it must do its mission.

And let no one say that there is no time for all of this: no time for wider interests, no time for further degrees, no time for secular organizations . . . Yes, of course we must ensure that we don't neglect our families, our prayers, our parishes or ourselves – but a stimulated mind makes for a better parish priest, so to pursue new interests should be a firm recommendation to every incumbent.

## Conclusion

This chapter has been a rather personal one. It tells you how *I* do it. We're all different, we all have different interests, and we are all in different situations. I might pack the day with 12 different activities. Another incumbent might spend it on one or two. What is essential is that both of us regularly reflect on what we're doing and why, and that we develop understandings of what skills we need and where we might find them. We will also both need support. We will each have different support networks; what matters is that we have them. We need them because it *isn't* all rosy, and because alongside every positive evaluation I have given of the role of the stipendiary incumbent there is a danger. For instance, the provision of housing in the parish – essential if the incumbent is to belong to the community the parish serves and is to be available to that community – means that the priest's family is far from secure. The priest's death, the priest's long-term illness, the priest's loss of faith, the breakdown of a marriage – these can all leave the family homeless. Yes, provision is made, but at just the point when everything else might be falling apart, the family home can disappear too, adding considerably to the insecurity. There really is no way round this, and it is an issue that anyone intending to be a stipendiary incumbent needs to be aware of. Rather deeper and perhaps less obvious is the stress imposed by being paid to have faith. We cannot be sure whether we believe the Christian faith because we're being paid or because we believe it. As with most issues, our motives are inextricably mixed, making it quite impossible even to begin the necessary internal discussion. So where does that leave our confession of faith? As a free act of the will? Or as to some extent coerced by our wishing to remain paid and housed?

The only means I have discovered to reduce the tension is to keep up my transferable skills. I know that I can always get another job if I need one. In my view every stipendiary incumbent should try to be in that position. It means that I can have some confidence that I am believing these things because I believe them, and that I am doing this task because it is still my vocation: it is the task to which God calls me.

And maybe at some point I shall no longer be a stipendiary priest. Maybe there will be another vocation, another absorbing task, another set of responsibilities. This too every stipendiary priest needs to know if they are to be committed, by an act of will, to the task of being a stipendiary incumbent.

And then of course there's the stress caused by the knowledge that next week there might be no one in the congregation. Whether we admit it or not, this fact is a cause of some anxiety – and maybe of greater anxiety because we *don't* admit it. On any particular Sunday morning, everyone except the incumbent is there because they choose to be (and in my experience this sometimes goes for the musician, too, even if they're being paid to be there); and next Sunday they might all choose *not* to be there. Here is another reason for making sure there's plenty of diversity in one's life, and plenty of options for the future. It helps to reduce the anxiety, which means that the incumbent is less likely to behave in ways that reduce people's desire to be there.

None of that diminishes in any way the privilege of being a stipendiary incumbent, with diverse roles in the community, the congregation, and the wider Church, and the freedom to explore ways of relating the gospel to an increasingly secular world. And the roles really are *very* diverse. In the congregation the incumbent is a member of a congregation, chair of its management committee, its paid servant, the president of its worship. If this were any other kind of charity then the Charity Commission would investigate the role conflicts, but in a Church of England parish the combination seems to be appropriate, and it seems to work. The diversity of roles is appropriate because the incumbent *is* a member of the congregation, *is* a representative of the Church universal, and *is* paid a stipend so that he or she has the time to involve themselves in whatever demands their attention. And the diversity is appropriate because congregations are unlike any other kind of organization. They are member organizations, but the boundary of the membership is unclear; they are autonomous yet related in a variety of ways to a diocese and to other parishes; and their responsibility is both undefined (as to the task) and tightly defined (in relation to geographical boundaries). And to this strange organization the incumbent belongs, and at the same time he or she has a leadership position within the congregation and in the community in which it is set.

So let's see an end to the dissolution of parish boundaries and the amalgamation of parishes. If we can't find or pay enough *stipendiary* incumbents then let's have *non*-stipendiary ones. This chapter contains sufficient reasons for doing so. And let's make sure that, whatever changes we see in the terms and conditions of the stipendiary clergy, they never become employees, with job descriptions and defined hours.

The office of incumbent is one of the glories of the Church of England. If ever we lose it we'll wish we hadn't.

## Further reading

Ramsey, Michael, *The Christian Priest Today*, SPCK, London, 1972.
Cocksworth, Christopher and Rosalind Brown, *Being a Priest Today: Exploring Priestly Identity*, Canterbury Press, London, 2002.

## Notes

1 I here use the term 'incumbent' loosely to cover priests-in-charge, team rectors and team vicars as well as clergy who have been inducted into the freehold of the benefice. Every parish has a stipendiary priest. It might be an incumbent: someone instituted to the living by the bishop (literally, 'the living': enough to live on) and inducted into the 'freehold' by the archdeacon – which means that they can stay in that post until they are 70. It might be a priest in charge – licensed to do the job, and paid, but with no security – though that might soon change under pressure from the government and following agreement in principle by the Church's General Synod to bring clergy terms and conditions of service more in line with those experienced by employees. It might be a team rector (who is a sort of incumbent, but with a fixed term licence rather than a permanent freehold), or a team vicar (again with a fixed term licence), members of teams of clergy serving a number of parishes or a number of districts in a single parish. The priest might have the care of one parish, or might have the care of several – and in rural areas and some urban areas it's now wise to phone before calling, because if the priest isn't in then it's a long wasted journey. I do not deal with the different kinds of tenure separately because soon there might

be only one kind of tenure for all clergy of the Church of England, with all of them subject for the first time to grievance, disciplinary and redundancy procedures.

2 The Ordinal, 1980, revised in 2000 (The Archbishops' Council of the Church of England, 2000). Unfortunately, the revision did not include the introduction of inclusive language.

# Conclusion
## Appropriately Diverse

But we appeal to you, brothers and sisters, to respect those who labour among you, and have charge of you in the Lord and admonish you; esteem them very highly in love because of their work. Be at peace among yourselves. (1 Thessalonians 5.12, 13)

The *Alternative Service Book* Ordinal describes the priest in terms of what they do:

A priest is called by God to work with the bishop and with his fellow-priests, as servant and shepherd among the people to whom he is sent. He is to proclaim the word of the Lord, to call his hearers to repentance, and in Christ's name to absolve and to declare the forgiveness of sins. He is to baptize and prepare the baptized for Confirmation. He is to preside at the celebration of the Holy Communion. He is to lead his people in prayer and worship, to intercede for them, to bless them in the name of the Lord, and to teach and encourage by word and example. He is to minister to the sick, and prepare the dying for their death. He must set the Good Shepherd always before him as the pattern of his calling, caring for the people committed to his charge, and joining with them in a common witness to the world.

In the name of our Lord we bid you remember the greatness of the trust now to be committed to your charge, about which you have been taught in your preparation for this ministry. You are to be messengers, watchmen, and stewards of the Lord; you are to teach and to admonish, to feed and to provide for the Lord's family, to search for his children in the wilderness of this world's temptations and to guide them through its confusions, so that they may be saved through Christ for ever.

Remember always with thanksgiving that the treasure now to be entrusted to you is Christ's own flock, bought through the shedding of his blood on the cross. The Church and congregation among whom you will serve are one with him: they are his body. Serve them with joy, build them up in faith, and do all in your power to bring them to loving obedience to Christ.[1]

In this book, representatives of a variety of ministries in the Church have told us what they *do*. These are our stories, and we hope that any reader who might be reflecting on their own vocation will find them helpful.

On the whole, the Church's licensed and other ministries are in good heart and there is no shortage of people testing their vocation to them (except for Licensed Lay Workers, in decline largely because many who in the past would have become LLWs are now priests, pastoral auxiliaries, social workers or community development workers).

But do we need *licensed* ministries? Does being a 'Reader', with a licence from the bishop, make someone any better at what they do? Not better, maybe, but it does make the Reader accountable to the Church, it gives the Church as a whole a responsibility to support and supervise a Reader's ministry, it makes expectations clearer, and it increases the Reader's confidence that what they're doing is the Church's work and not just their own.

So the next question must be: Which ministries should be licensed and which not? Parish musicians are appointed locally, and the many ministries listed by Ann Atkins are recognized and resourced locally, not nationally.

Maybe a related question is this: To what extent does the minister speak for the Church beyond the boundaries of the congregation? In their communities and in their places of work Readers, Southwark Pastoral Auxiliaries, Church Army

officers and clergy might be expected to do so, so a licence
is appropriate. A lay worker managing a church community
project (as Gillian Reeve has done) might be expected to represent the Church to secular authorities, so licensing might be
appropriate here, too. Similarly, youth workers speak for the
Church in contemporary youth culture, so maybe licensing
would be appropriate for them.

A related issue is that of qualifications. Most church youth
workers now have secular youth work qualifications, and
Ordained Local Ministers now normally receive a diploma
on completing their training. There is a case for secular
qualifications being both recognized by licensing and required
for licensing. This strengthens the case for licensing youth
workers and also suggests that trained community workers
working on behalf of the Church should be licensed (LCW:
Licensed Community Worker).

A second question raised by this book is that of who should
be paid for what they do. Stipendiary clergy and Church Army
officers receive stipends, and many parish musicians are paid
by the parishes in which they work. Readers and Southwark
Pastoral Auxiliaries are not paid. Many youth workers are
paid, but some not. Chaplains are paid by the institutions
they work for or by the Church – or not, as in the case of many
workplace chaplains. This untidy situation is likely to continue. On the whole, if a ministry is regarded as *necessary* then
it will be paid for. So musicians and youth workers might be
paid, and some clergy will be. Ministry that is beneficial but
not regarded as necessary for the maintenance of the Church's
core activities will remain voluntary, so Readers and pastoral
auxiliaries will only be paid if there are insufficient clergy to
manage the necessary pastoral and liturgical tasks – and not
necessarily then if they'll work for nothing, which of course
many are happy to do.

For what this book shows is how much commitment to the
task can be found among ordinary ministers in ordinary places.
All of the licensed or commissioned contributors, and those
they have consulted, regard their licences or commissionings

as starting points, not as possessions. They put in hours of sometimes draining hard work; they struggle with such large themes as the reconciliation of the sacred and the secular; and they regard their ministries as belonging to God and to the Church and not to themselves. And those ministers recruited and resourced locally – children's church teachers, youth workers, musicians, and all those listed in Chapter 2 – are people offering commitment, skills and enthusiasm, and they too put in long hours of hard work.

And what this book also shows is the diversity of gifts brought to these ministries. Every minister, whether licensed or not, brings to their vocation the talents, time and commitment God has given to them. This means that what we hear in the contributors' chapters are particular ways of being a Reader, a Licensed Lay Worker, a musician, a chaplain . . . So there will be considerable diversity in the ways in which these ministries will be exercised, and lots of overlap between one ministry and another. A Non-stipendiary Minister with a gift for youth work will do youth work, and a youth worker might have a gift for music and co-ordinate a parish's music group. Boundaries are blurred. Because licensed ministries need to be accountable they need to have some definite character and a list of expected tasks, and we shall have to live with the tension between stated expectations and the diverse and overlapping practice of which this book is evidence. The Church needs to train people for the prescribed functions of the licensed ministries and also to support them in their diverse practice.

In the end, this book is less about ministries than it is about ministry: God's people serving God's world and God's Church. For this ministry we give thanks, and to it we commit ourselves.

## Note

1 The Ordinal, 1980, revised in 2000 (The Archbishops' Council of the Church of England, 2000). Unfortunately, the revision did not include the introduction of inclusive language.

# Glossary

Accredited ministry — A ministry recognized by the bishop of a diocese by the granting of a licence or commission.

Acolyte — An adult or child who assists a priest at the altar. They will often carry candles in procession at the beginning and end of a service and during the Gospel procession. Usually accompanied by a crucifer.

Admission to communion — In the Diocese of Southwark, and in various other dioceses, parishes have permission to admit children to communion before they are confirmed if they are baptized, over seven years of age and have attended a course of preparation.

Advent — Traditionally a penitential season, starting on the fourth Sunday before Christmas and ending on Christmas Eve. Now the period during which Christmas is celebrated.

Advisory Council for the Church's Ministry (ACCM) — A council that advised the bishops on training for ministry and ran selection conferences to enable it to recommend candidates to the bishops for ordination. It was replaced by the Advisory Board for Ministry (ABM), which has now been replaced by the Ministry Division.

All age worship | Worship attended by people of all ages, including children, and during which at various points there will be activities accessible to people of all ages.

Alpha course | A course of study for enquirers published by Holy Trinity, Brompton. The course consists of a series of evenings on which participants share a meal, listen to a talk, and hold a discussion. There is also a weekend about the Holy Spirit.

Altar | A table at which, according to Jesus' command, bread and wine are taken, thanks is given, bread is broken, and the bread and wine are shared. It is called an altar because the stone construction on which animals were slaughtered during and before the time of Jesus was called an altar.

Amen | This word, from the Hebrew via Greek, means 'so be it', so is often said by a congregation at the end of a prayer offered by an individual to denote the congregation's agreement to what has been prayed. Frequently now said at the end of prayers spoken by the whole congregation.

| | |
|---|---|
| Anglican | The Anglican Communion is all those dioceses that are in communion with the Archbishop of Canterbury – in practice, all those whose bishops attend the Lambeth Conference once every ten years. |
| Anglicanism | A set of practices and ideas that characterize the Anglican Communion or more specifically the Church of England. |
| Annual Parochial Church Meeting (APCM) | A meeting held each year (before the end of April) at which members of the Electoral Roll vote for the Parochial Church Council, receive the accounts, and undertake other business similar to that of Annual General Meetings in other organizations. Churchwardens are also elected at the meeting. |
| Applied theology | Theology applied to something in the real world. |
| Archbishops' Council | A council chaired by the Archbishops of Canterbury and York, which was set up to streamline the government of the Church of England. |
| Archdeacon | A bishop's assistant, with legal and other functions of their own but which can be delegated. The archdeacon must be in deacon's orders, but is usually a priest. In practice the archdeacon can be a pastoral figure in the diocese. |
| Archdeaconry | An area in which an archdeacon is the archdeacon. |

| | |
|---|---|
| Area dean | A new name for a rural dean. |
| Baptism | The initiation rite for a Christian. It can be carried out at any age, but when a child is baptized godparents speak for them. |
| Baptist | A denomination that believes only adults can be baptized. Also used to designate a member of that denomination. |
| Benefice | A parish or parishes of which a priest is incumbent. |
| Bishop | Someone ordained by other bishops to the first order of the Church's threefold ministry of bishop, priest and deacon. The bishop acts as a focus of unity for the diocese and cares for its people and clergy. |
| Canons | 'Canon' has two meanings: a) the title of a cathedral dignitary, either residentiary (i.e. receiving a stipend to work on the cathedral's staff) or honorary (i.e. receiving a stipend for some other post but having the right to sit in a cathedral stall); b) a rule governing the Church. The canons are revised by General Synod and agreed by Parliament. |
| Catholic | When with 'Roman', see 'Roman Catholic' below. When with 'Anglican', as in 'Anglo-Catholic', it means a member of the Church of England who prefers a more elaborate liturgy and holds beliefs Roman Catholics hold. When with |

'liberal', as in 'liberal catholic',
it means someone who prefers a
simpler liturgy and believes some
of what Anglo-Catholics believe. In
the historic creeds the word means
'universal'.

| | |
|---|---|
| Chalice | A large cup, usually of silver or silver plated, into which wine is poured at the Eucharist and from which the congregation drinks. |
| Chamber of Commerce | A gathering of business men and women from a particular borough or area to enable them to do business with each other. |
| Chaplain | Someone fulfilling a pastoral role in an institution, usually a hospital, factory, university, etc. The chaplain might or might not be a member of the clergy. |
| Chapter | A regular meeting of the clergy of a deanery that they are expected, but not obliged, to attend. |
| Child protection | The protection of children from physical, mental, sexual and spiritual abuse. Hence 'child protection policy': a list of dos and don'ts designed to protect both children and the adults looking after them; and 'child protection officer': someone whose job it is to enforce the dos and prevent the don'ts and to listen to and act on accusations of abuse. |

Children's church | What a church's children and children's church teachers do while the Sunday morning service is happening. Different age groups often meet in different rooms, and activities might include prayer, singing, listening to biblical and other stories, cutting things out, gluing things, and colouring in pictures.

Christian Aid | A charity that funds development work in poor countries and campaigns for global justice. During Christian Aid Week, which is always during May, a stunningly committed group of people knock on people's doors and ask them for money.

Church | With a lower-case initial letter it means a congregation of Christians or the building within which they meet. With a capital initial letter it means the entire universal body of Christian believers and all of its local manifestations. The word can also have a capital letter if it is part of a denomination's title, as in 'Methodist Church'.
In many contexts in this book the word will start with a capital letter because it is short for 'Church of England'. The word also has a sociological meaning: see below, 'denomination'.

Church Army | A voluntary hierarchical organization that evangelizes, runs homelessness projects, and generally lives out the gospel. Best understood as the Anglican version of the Salvation Army. Hence 'Church Army evangelist': 'evangelist' because they are commissioned as evangelists; and 'Church Army officer', which means 'Church Army evangelist'.

Church of England | A federation of dioceses in England that have bishops in communion with the Archbishop of Canterbury, and, since dioceses are federations of parishes with umbrella organizations to serve them, the Church of England is a federation of parishes and of umbrella organisations.

Church representation rules | Rules established by General Synod to govern elections to and meetings of Parochial Church Councils and Deanery and Diocesan Synods.

*Church Times* | An independent newspaper carrying news and opinion about the Church of England. Excellent cartoons.

Churches together | Many areas have 'Churches together' groups to which congregations of different denominations send representatives. These groups might or might not be formally constituted. There is usually a regular meeting of representatives of churches in the area, and joint projects might be planned.

| | |
|---|---|
| Church Urban Fund | Following the publication of the 'Faith in the City' report in 1985 the Church Urban Fund was set up to fund community development projects in Urban Priority Areas. |
| Churchwarden | An ancient elected office. Each parish has two churchwardens elected annually. The churchwardens have a number of powers, such as the ability to veto the appointment of an incumbent, and a number of responsibilities, such as the annual completion of articles of enquiry sent by the archdeacon. They are responsible, with the incumbent, for the maintenance of public worship and the care of the church building. |
| Clergy | A collective noun for bishops, priests and deacons. Whether the clergy remain laypeople is an interesting question. A priest remains a deacon, and a bishop remains a priest and a deacon, so it might be thought that they all remain laypeople. But the Church's synodical structure separates people into bishops, other clergy, and laity. |
| Common Worship | The name of the collection of alternative services authorized for use in the Church of England in 2000. |
| Communion | Sharing in bread and wine at the Eucharist, from which derives the meaning of 'taking communion to . . .' – usually to someone who can't |

get out and to whom a priest or someone else takes bread and wine from the service in church. See also 'Anglican'.

Confirmation
The bishop lays his hands on the candidate's head and prays for the Holy Spirit to 'confirm' them. Historically this action was part of a single baptismal rite. Confirmation is either administered to people who were baptized as infants and now wish to 'confirm' the promises previously made on their behalf, or it immediately follows baptism as an adult. Normally only people who are confirmed (or are ready to be confirmed) receive communion. But now members of other denominations are also welcome to receive communion. See above on 'admission to communion'.

Congregation
Any gathering of Christians for the purpose of worship.

Conventional district
An area within one or more parishes under the care of a minister. When such a district is established the parishes within which it lies lose most of their functions in relation to the district. Conventional districts are established where new housing and other developments occur and it isn't initially clear how parish boundaries should be reorganized.

Crucifer
He or she carries a cross at the front of a liturgical procession at

the beginning or end of a service or during a procession before the Gospel reading is read. Usually accompanied by acolytes.

Curacy

An assistant priest's post. An assistant priest in a parish can be either stipendiary or non-stipendiary. The term often applies to an ordained minister's first and training post where the curate is under the supervision of a training incumbent. For the first year the curate is a deacon and thereafter a priest.

Curate

Someone undertaking a curacy.

Daughter church

A building and congregation established in another part of the parish by the 'mother church'. Sometimes the daughter gets bigger than the mother.

Deacon

Someone ordained by the bishop to the third order of the Church's threefold ministry of bishop, priest and deacon. The deacon's role is outlined in the Ordinal and is one of service and teaching. The deacon cannot preside at the Eucharist or be incumbent of a parish.

Deanery

An area, sometimes coterminous with a natural community or communities but not always, usually comprising a dozen or so parishes. Every deanery has a Deanery Synod (chaired by the Lay Chair and the rural dean) and a clergy chapter (chaired by the rural dean).

| | |
|---|---|
| Deanery Synod | The governing body of a deanery. |
| Denomination | A federation of congregations, usually with an umbrella organization or organizations to fulfil functions best carried out centrally, such as the payment of clergy. The word also has a separate but connected meaning in the social sciences, where it means a category of religious organization between the categories of 'sect' and 'church'. The denomination has more open boundaries than a sect, but boundaries less open than for a church (with 'church' here defined in terms of characteristics such as open boundaries and diverse belief-systems, i.e., not as defined above). |
| Diocesan missioner | Either a canon of the cathedral or someone else whose job it is to remind the parishes that mission is their responsibility. They might do some mission themselves. |
| Diocesan Synod | The governing body of a diocese. There are three houses: bishops, clergy, and laity. A vote by houses can be requested. The synod sets diocesan policy and the budget of the diocese. All bishops in the diocese are members, and there are elections for the house of clergy (among all clergy) and for the house of laity (the electors being Deanery Synod members). |

| | |
|---|---|
| Diocese | A federation of parishes with an umbrella organization to carry out those functions best dealt with centrally, such as the payment of clergy. The chief pastor of a diocese is its bishop (who might be assisted by suffragan or area bishops). |
| Diocese of Southwark | The parishes of south London and of parts of Kent and Surrey. |
| Director of Ordinands | Someone who encourages people to explore vocations to the ordained ministry, pilots them through the selection process, keeps in touch during their training, and allocates them to curacies. |
| District | In a parish with more than one church building districts can be established. The Parochial Church Council can delegate to District Church Councils certain decisions relating to particular buildings, the congregation that meets in it, and the Church's mission in the community in which the building is situated. |
| District Church Council | The governing body of a district. The Parochial Church Council of the parish in which the district lies decides which decisions to delegate to the District Church Council. |
| Ecumenical Borough Deans | In London Boroughs, and elsewhere, each denomination appoints a Borough Dean to represent the denomination to the local authority and other parts of civil society. The borough deans meet, and often act together. |

Ecumenism

The relating of different denominations to each other at local, regional or national level.

Elder

The churches Paul and others founded during the first Christian century were governed by elders: older respected members of the congregation. Some denominations retain this name for those who govern a congregation.

Electoral roll

A list of all those who fill in a form to say they want to be on the roll. Anyone who lives in the parish or who worships regularly in the parish church can be on the roll. It's the nearest thing the Church of England has got to a membership list. In order to fill in the form you have to declare yourself to be a member of the Church of England or of a church in communion with it.

Episcopal area

Part of a diocese in which some of the diocesan bishop's functions have been delegated to an area bishop.

Eucharist

A fourfold action of taking bread and wine, giving thanks over them, breaking the bread, and sharing the bread and wine. The word's meaning generally extends to the whole event, including hymns, readings, prayers, the Peace, etc.

Evangelical

A Christian or a congregation might be called evangelical if they think of the Bible as the Christian's primary authority. Evangelical worship is often informal.

| | |
|---|---|
| Evangelist | Someone who tells the good news of the Kingdom of God's coming. |
| Evening Prayer | An evening service containing Bible readings, canticles (biblical passages said by the congregation), and prayers. |
| Evensong | Evening Prayer with some parts sung, and maybe hymns added. |
| Faculty | A document giving a parish permission to alter the parish church or to undertake a particular activity within it. |
| Faith community | Any body of people who are adherents of a religion. |
| Free Church | This term normally designates any denomination apart from the Church of England and the Roman Catholic Church, e.g., the Methodist Church. There are many non-affiliated congregations that can be regarded as free churches in their own right. |
| Freehold | A priest who is inducted as rector or vicar (or team rector) holds the freehold of the benefice. This is a useful legal fiction. It means that the incumbent owns the parish church and the parsonage house but can't do anything with them except look after them. (A priest who holds the freehold can stay in post until they are 70 years old.) |

General Synod | The national governing body of the Church of England. There are three houses: bishops, clergy (but not bishops), and laity. A measure has to pass in all three houses if a vote by houses is requested. The synod sets national policy and the budget of the Church's central departments. All diocesan bishops are members, and there are elections for the house of clergy (among all clergy) and for the house of laity (the electors being Deanery Synod members).

Healing ministry | Praying for people who are ill or otherwise suffering, the prayer often being accompanied by the laying on of hands and/or anointing with oil.

Higher education | Education of a more academic nature for people over 18 years of age.

Holy Communion | See 'Eucharist'.

Holy Spirit | The third person of the Trinity. For this and other theological terms readers should consult a good theological dictionary.

House of bishops | The term can either mean all the bishops who sit in a particular synod, or just the diocesan bishops.

House of clergy | The members of clergy elected to a synod, apart from the bishops, who have a house of their own.

House of laity | The members of the laity elected to a synod. Clergy cannot be members of the house of laity even if they might still be members of the laity.

| | |
|---|---|
| Incumbent | The priest who holds the freehold of the benefice. |
| Industrial chaplain | A chaplain in an industrial institution, though in practice many industrial chaplains undertake a variety of activities in connection with the Christian faith's relationship to the economy. |
| Industrial mission | The activity of relating the Christian faith to the world of work and to the economy. An industrial mission is an institution set up for this purpose. |
| Inter-Diocesan Certificate | A certificate offered by colleges with a Christian foundation to students training as social workers, youth workers, and in some other professions, the certificate being recognized by all bishops as a qualification that might lead to a licence to preach being granted. |
| Intercessions | Prayers, normally offered during public worship, requesting God to do things. |
| Inter-faith | A description of worship or other activity in which institutions and/ or members of different faiths are involved. Because inter-faith activity such as joint worship might distress members of individual faith communities, such activity tends to be small-scale and for individuals committed to inter-faith work. |

| | |
|---|---|
| Laity | Anyone other than bishops, priests and deacons. Whether bishops, priests and deacons remain laity after their ordination is an interesting question. |
| Lambeth Conference | A conference convened once every ten years to which the Archbishop of Canterbury invites every bishop whom he believes to be in communion with him. |
| Lay chair | Parochial Church Councils and synods have clerical chairs and lay chairs. In the case of the PCC the lay chair only chairs when the clerical chair isn't present. In synods lay and clerical chairs usually alternate. |
| Lay Reader | An old name for a Reader. |
| Layperson | A member of the laity. |
| Lent | A penitential season of approximately six weeks before Easter. |
| Licence | A document giving a deacon, priest or Reader permission to fulfil their ministry in a particular parish or parishes. |
| Licensed Lay Worker | A member of the laity who is licensed to preach, often following the granting of an interdiocesan certificate. |
| Liturgy | What is said and done at church services. |

| | |
|---|---|
| Local Ecumenical Partnership | A formally constituted relationship between churches (buildings and/or congregations) of different denominations. Provision is often made for joint worship within certain limits. |
| London City Mission | An independent mission organization that employs evangelists to tell the good news of Jesus Christ to Londoners. Evangelists are sometimes attached to parishes. |
| Lord's Supper | See 'Eucharist'. |
| Magi | The real Greek name for the wise men who came to see the child Jesus. |
| Mass | See 'Eucharist'. |
| Measure | Legislation passed by General Synod and approved by Parliament. |
| Methodist Church | A denomination started by some of John Wesley's followers. |
| Minister | A rather loose term to refer to anyone undertaking a liturgical or pastoral function. The minister can be a bishop, a priest, a deacon, a Reader, a Southwark Pastoral Auxiliary, or a layperson. |
| Minister in Secular Employment (MSE) | A non-stipendiary priest who sees, the focus of their ministry in their place of work rather than in the parish to which they are licensed. |
| Ministry Division | See the 'Advisory Council for the Church's Ministry'. |
| Mission | Going out to serve and evangelize. Hence 'mission team': a group of people in a parish or diocese trained and commissioned to do mission. |

| | |
|---|---|
| Missionary | Someone who does mission. |
| Morning Prayer | A morning service containing Bible readings, canticles (biblical passages said by the congregation), and prayers. |
| Mother church | See 'daughter church'. |
| Multi-faith | A description of activity in which institutions and/or members of different faiths are involved. Unlike 'inter-faith', joint activities that might distress members of the faith communities involved are avoided. |
| Muslim | An adherent of Islam, the religion founded on the Quran and of which Mohammed is the final prophet. |
| Night Prayer | A late evening service containing Bible readings, canticles (biblical passages said by the congregation), and prayers. (Also called Compline.) |
| Non-stipendiary Minister (NSM) | A deacon or priest who does not receive a stipend. Most non-stipendiary clergy are curates and are usually designated 'honorary curate'. |
| Office | Morning Prayer and Evening Prayer are offices. |
| To ordain | To make someone a deacon, priest or bishop. See 'ordination' below. |
| Ordained Local Minister (OLM) | A minister ordained deacon and then priest following a diocesan training course. The licence usually restricts the minister's role to a particular parish or parishes. |

| Ordination | The act of making someone a deacon, priest or bishop. This is done by the bishop (or, in the case of the ordination of a bishop, bishops) laying hands on the candidate and praying that God's Spirit will give them the necessary grace for the office and work of the ministry in question. |
|---|---|
| Parish | The parish is a patch of land with its community and institutions, with a congregation or congregations, with a priest or priests, and with a building or buildings for worship. |
| Parish Communion | See 'Eucharist'. |
| Parish musician | Someone appointed by the parish to co-ordinate the music. |
| Parochial Church Council (PCC) | The governing body of a parish. The churchwardens and the incumbent are *ex officio* members. Members are elected from the electoral roll at the Annual Parochial Church Meeting. The council takes all decisions relating to the life of the parish except for a few reserved to the incumbent (mainly in relation to the conduct of worship). |
| Pastoral | Anything to do with the care of the parish's people, or with the parish's organization or boundaries, or with the structures within which clergy operate. Hence 'pastoral auxiliary' – someone appointed to do pastoral work. |
| Pentecost | A Jewish festival. At the Pentecost immediately following Jesus' |

resurrection the Holy Spirit
descended on the apostles and the
Christian Church was born.

Pentecostal

A description of congregations
or federations in which the
spiritual gifts mentioned by Paul
in 1 Corinthians 12 and 14 (and
particularly speaking in tongues) are
central to prayer and worship.

Permission to
officiate (PTO)

A bishop's authorization of a priest
to preside and preach in his diocese.
Retired clergy are usually granted
permission to officiate, and some
others are too.

Presbyter

Greek word for elder.

Priest

Someone ordained by the bishop
to the second order of the Church's
threefold ministry of bishop, priest
and deacon. The priest's functions
are outlined in the Ordinal.

Priest-in-charge

A priest appointed to a parish either
with a fixed-term licence or with no
security at all, so less in charge than
a priest with the freehold.

Purificator

Small linen cloth for wiping the
chalice between communicants.

Quiet day

A day during which there are
periods of silence, often interspersed
with talks or services.

Reader

Someone trained in preaching
and in leading worship (but not
the Eucharist) and licensed by the
bishop to fulfil these functions in a
parish or parishes.

| | |
|---|---|
| Rector | One of the two designations of an incumbent of a parish. The other is 'vicar'. Historically the vicar stood in for a rector. |
| Registrar | The diocese's solicitor who deals with leases, elections to General Synod, and other legal matters. |
| Requiem Mass | A Mass to remember and pray for the dead. |
| Retreat | A period for reflection, often away from home. |
| Roman Catholic Church | A federation of parishes and dioceses in communion with the Bishop of Rome. |
| Rural dean | A priest appointed by the bishop to convene the clergy chapter and chair the Deanery Synod. There is some debate as to whether the rural dean is the bishop's representative to the deanery or the deanery's representative to the bishop. He or she is usually in practice a bit of both. |
| Sacrament | An outward and visible sign of an inward spiritual reality. The Church of England recognizes two sacraments: baptism and the Eucharist. Other churches recognize rather more. |
| Sacristan | Someone who prepares the altar, linen, vessels, bread and wine, etc. for the Eucharist and cares for linen and vessels. An important office. |

| | |
|---|---|
| The South East Institute for Theological Education (SEITE) | A part-time training course for the ordained ministry serving the dioceses of Southwark, Canterbury, Rochester and Chichester, and also the Methodist and United Reformed Churches. It replaced the Southwark Ordination Course. |
| Sidesperson | Someone elected at the Annual Parochial Church Meeting to assist the churchwardens in welcoming people to services, taking the collection, guiding people as they receive communion, and counting the money. |
| Southwark Ordination Course | A part-time training course for the ordained ministry established in 1962 for the Diocese of Southwark. It was replaced by SEITE. |
| Southwark Pastoral Auxiliary (SPA) | Someone trained in pastoral work and authorized by the bishop to serve in a parish or parishes in the Diocese of Southwark. |
| Spirituality | That aspect of our lives we might call spiritual. |
| Stewardship | Offering to God and to the Church our time, talents and money. Hence 'stewardship campaign'. |
| Stipend | What parochial clergy are paid. It is not a salary as there is no contract of employment. The payment is intended to enable the priest and their family to live without anxiety and thus to be of service to the parish. |

| | |
|---|---|
| Synod | A gathering of elected and *ex officio* members for deliberation and decision-making. The Church of England has synods at the parish level (Parochial Church Council), the deanery level (Deanery Synod), the diocesan level (Diocesan Synod), and the national level (General Synod). |
| Synodical | Anything to do with synods. |
| Team ministry | A team of clergy, comprising a team rector and team vicar(s), serving a parish or parishes. The team rector is the incumbent, and the team vicar(s) are not. They are all told that they are of incumbent status. |
| Team rector | Every team ministry has a team rector who is expected to fulfil a co-ordinating role. The team rector holds the freehold of the benefice for a limited period, usually for seven years. The team rector is not a rector. |
| Team vicar | Every team ministry has one or more team vicars. A team vicar is of 'incumbent status', as is the team rector. The team vicar is not a vicar but can be designated vicar of a particular parish or district. |
| Thames Gateway | A great deal of empty land ripe for development on both sides of the Thames estuary along with existing communities adjacent to it. In south London the Thames Gateway includes Thamesmead, Woolwich, |

|  | the north end of Charlton and the Greenwich Peninsula. |
|---|---|
| Theology | Words about God. |
| Title | That part of a curacy which has to be completed before a priest can be appointed to a post with responsibility. Usually two years for a stipendiary curate and four years for a non-stipendiary curate or Ordained Local Minister. |
| United Reformed Church | A Free Church formed in 1972 from a merger of the Congregational Church and the Presbyterian Church in England. |
| Vicar | One of the two designations of an incumbent of a parish. The other is 'rector'. Historically the vicar stood in for a rector. (A team vicar or a team rector can also be designated vicar of a parish or a district even though neither is a vicar or a rector.) |
| Vocation | A sense of being called by God to a particular task. Often the word on its own refers to a vocation to be a priest, but it shouldn't. |
| Word and sacrament | The two main aspects of a priest's liturgical role: preaching God's word and presiding at the sacraments of baptism and the Eucharist. |
| Word, service of the | A service of readings, prayers, hymns and sermon, but no Eucharist. |

| | |
|---|---|
| Worker priest | Now known as Minister in Secular Employment. |
| Workplace chaplain | A chaplain in places where people work. Workplace chaplains used to be called industrial chaplains when there was more industry. |
| Worship leader | Someone who leads all or part of a service. It often denotes someone who introduces worship songs and offers commentary between them. They might or might not be ordained. |
| Wychcroft | The Southwark Diocesan Training Centre – a wonderful old house in a marvellous setting in Surrey. |
| Youth for Christ | A voluntary organization that evangelizes among young people. |
| Youth worker | Someone who runs activities for young people or simply gets to know them and listens to them. |